Story of the 36th

The Experiences of the 36th Division in World War One

By Capt. Ben H. Chastaine

Published by Pantianos Classics

ISBN-13: 978-1-78987-485-3

First published in 1920

Capt. Ben H. Chastaine

Contents

Foreword v

Chapter One - Organization and Training - Fort Sill and Camp Bowie 6

Chapter Two - From Camp Bowie to Brest and Redon ... 18

Chapter Three - Training in France 26

Chapter Four - To the Front 32

Chapter Five - St. Etienne 48

Chapter Six - St. Etienne — (Continued) 71

Chapter Seven - St. Etienne and After 84

Chapter Eight - The General Advance 100

Chapter Nine - Forest Ferme 110

Chapter Ten - To Bar-Le-Duc — the Armistice 121

Chapter Eleven - Operations of the 111th Engineers .. 127

Chapter Twelve - Home Again 131

The Honor Roll 141

Killed in Action 141

Died of Wounds 151

Foreword

When the old First Regiment, Oklahoma National Guard, went to the Mexican border in 1916, Captain Ben H. Chastaine was with the outfit as a second lieutenant. He had been a reporter for The Daily Oklahoman and so he was asked to keep the newspaper in touch with the home boys on the Rio Grande. He did it well. When America's participation in the World War became a reality, the First Regiment, then federalized, was the first Oklahoma organization that went into the service. During the first six months of training the regiment was at Fort Sill, Oklahoma, later being consolidated with some Texas companies to form the 142nd Regiment of the Thirty-sixth division, which trained at Camp Bowie, Texas. Chastaine reported the development of the unit into a vigorous fighting force in the clear narrative of a finished reporter. He received the commission to keep The Daily Oklahoman informed of the doings of the "old first Oklahoma" overseas and he did it as well as he did his share of the fighting. Chastaine's dispatches from France were printed in a series of full-page stories in the Sunday edition of *The Daily Oklahoman*. Chastaine was promoted on the field of battle for valor. He went through until Armistice Day and remained with the 142nd until it started for port to ship for home. Then Chastaine was honored with a post in a regular army outfit that remained overseas many months. He retained his grade as captain and is at present an officer in the regular army stationed at Camp Zachary Taylor, Kentucky.

The Daily Oklahoman gladly gives its permission to the rewriting and publication of Chastaine's dispatches in book form. The bound volumes of a daily newspaper pass from the view of the public, but the vivid narrative of Oklahoma's heroic manhood, penned by the accurate and colorful Chastaine, deserves a place on the bookshelf of every Oklahoman.

Walter M. Harrison,
Managing Editor
The Daily Oklahoma

Chapter One - Organization and Training - Fort Sill and Camp Bowie

Where the barren stretches of the Champagne country spread out northward to blend with the fertile valley of the Aisne; where the planted pine and wiry grass grow meagerly in the chalky earth; where the shell-scarred ground upturns in sickly defiance of any growing thing; there where the warriors of Europe have battled since the days of Charlemagne, the soldiers of Texas and Oklahoma have left an imprint in the soil of France that will remain long after those who grimly stamped it have passed in their final review. Even though the name of the Thirty-sixth Division may pass from the organizations of the United States Army, it will not be forgotten by the firesides of northern France. Liberated French fathers and mothers will tell liberated sons and daughters of the onslaught of "le Trente-sixieme Division Americaine," in October 1918, when the soldiers from the American plains swept the "boche" invaders backward over the river, returning to France many miles of territory and many villages that had been under the rule of the tyrant for more than four miserable years.

The National Guard units of Texas and Oklahoma were among the first to be mobilized by the War Department following the declaration that a state of war existed between the United States and Germany in the spring of 1917. The First Oklahoma Infantry immediately was assembled at Fort Sill, Oklahoma, while the Second, Third and Fourth Texas Infantry regiments were sent to the Mexican border, where they as well as the Oklahoma Infantry had been on duty for many months previous. The actual declaration that war was in existence was published a day or two after some of these units had reached their stations. Preparations for this mobilization had been in progress about ten days before the movement began. Some of the Texas infantrymen had no more than returned to their homes after long service on the border than they were called upon to once more get into the uniform and take up military duty.

At this time the Oklahoma National Guard was composed of one infantry regiment, one troop of cavalry, the nucleus for a company of engineers, for an ambulance company and a field hospital company. All of these organizations had seen service on the border during the year previous, and contained seasoned troops. The Texas National Guard was made up of the infantry regiments already named, the First Squadron of cavalry. Battery A of the First Texas Artillery, Companies A and B of the First Texas Engineers, and Field Hospital Company No. 1. Most of these were made up of troops who had seen considerable service. The infantry regiments were organized at the close of the Spanish-American war and the other units had all served the year previous along the Mexican border. The Texas troops composed a brigade under the command of a brigadier general and his staff.

Upon arrival of the Oklahoma Infantry at Fort Sill, a schedule of intensive training that kept the men in the field throughout the day was taken up and continued through the entire summer. Instructors at the School of Musketry, then located at Fort Sill, planned the details of the regiment's training and assisted in bringing the officers and men to a point of efficiency. At the time, hopes were entertained by the personnel of the command that it would form a part of a composite division which would be among the first troops to be sent overseas. At one time information was received at the post that the transportation to take the regiment east, where it would be mobilized as a part of the "Rainbow" division, was on its way to Fort Sill, but this information proved to be groundless. However, to keep the command at a high point of efficiency and to maintain its full strength, in order to take advantage of such an opportunity, recruiting parties were sent to all parts of the state so that, in spite of the frequent discharge of soldiers having dependents, the regiment retained its maximum strength.

Breaking Ground for Trenches at Fort Sill.

In the training of the infantry the troops were taken into the field to construct trenches, modeled after those along the western front in Europe, and bayonet practice was a part of the daily program. The machine gun company was instructed in the use of the various types of machine gun then employed in the schools at the post and used the weapons on the range. The rifle companies also fired the prescribed course on the range. The pistol range was utilized as well. The hardest part of this training program was the trench construction m the sun-baked soil of the prairie. It was impossible to drive a pick more than an inch or two into the ground. The progress was slow and painful but the results accomplished gave an excellent conception of actual fire trenches, support trenches and reserve trenches with deep communications.

While the Oklahomans were in training at Fort Sill, the Texans along the border were getting their regularly established organizations in condition. There the troops were used for guard duty for the most part but some time was found for training purposes. Constant tours of guard duty brought about a fine discipline within the commands. Actual conditions replaced theory, but there was no construction of trenches along the plans taken up later. During this time these regiments also found recruits to fill their ranks to the required strength and trained them in the first lessons of a soldier on the banks of the Rio Grande.

While these older guard organizations were undergoing this period of training new organizations were being recruited in both states. In Texas a great drive for enough units to complete an entire Lone Star division was carried out with the result that the larger state was far more successful than the smaller one. In Texas four new infantry regiments were completed. These were the First Texas Infantry, recruited from the southwestern part of the state, where the Second Texas Infantry originally was organized; the Fifth Texas Infantry from the southeastern part of the state, where had originated the Third Texas Infantry; the Sixth Texas Infantry from the north and north-central portions of the state, in the same general area where the Fourth Texas Infantry had been recruited; and the Seventh Texas Infantry from the Panhandle country, virgin soil. The old Texas Artillery units were increased to two complete regiments of field artillery and the cavalry squadron was brought up to regimental proportions. In addition a battalion of engineers was formed as also had been a supply train, a field signal battalion, two ambulance companies and a field hospital company. All of these were recruited to the strength then required.

In Oklahoma three companies, or a complete battalion, of engineers also had been recruited and held in readiness for mobilization. Besides these a squadron of cavalry, a field hospital company and an ambulance company were completed. This ambulance company as well as the Texas supply train later was sent to Mineola, Long Island, to become a part of the Forty-second or "Rainbow" Division, and served throughout the war with that command. All of these organizations had a nucleus of former service men who aided materially later in developing the recruits.

While this recruiting was going forward in both states the troops along the border were getting restless in the belief that they were to be left in that situation while other troops over the country would be sent to Europe. The same rumors were current among the troops at Fort Sill. These were the events that transpired from the time the state of war was declared until five months later the first contingents of troops began to arrive at Camp Bowie, near Fort Worth, Texas, and the first tasks of organizing the Thirty-sixth Division were taken up.

Camp Bowie was well located on the hills about two and a half miles to the west of Fort Worth in that suburb of the city called Arlington Heights and on the road from Fort Worth to Weatherford, Texas. The site was ideal from the standpoint of drainage, as it was higher than any part of Fort Worth and was rolling so that water ran off it rapidly. The wind and dust that developed after the troops had been stationed there for a short time however created discomfort in many ways, although those of the older men who had been serving in the sandy country along the border of the arid region around Fort Sill, found the new camp pleasant in the extreme. When the camp was opened to troops the last week in August, 1917, it was not complete in some areas, no roads having been constructed and the water not being connected in the more remote portions of the reservation. This difficulty was overcome within a short time, in respect to the water supply, but it was many months before the roads were completed.

Company G, 1st Oklahoma Infantry at Camp Bowie.

Major General Edwin St. John Greble, from the Coast Artillery Corps, was selected to command the newly mobilized division, and his staff for the most part was made up of other officers from the regular army. His chief of staff was Colonel E. J. Williams. Other officers were Lieutenant Colonel R. F. Metcalfe, division surgeon; Major J. S. Upham, assistant chief of staff; Major E. F. Graham, division adjutant; Major J. V. Kuznik, division ordnance officer; Major Paul M. Goodrich, division signal officer; Major John P. Hasson, division quartermaster; and Major Harry S. Grier, division inspector. Most of these officers reached the camp shortly after General Greble arrived, August 25, and about that time Brigadier General George Blakely, also of the regular army, arrived to take command of the division's artillery.

First to arrive at the new camp were the engineer units from Oklahoma, under the command of Major Frank B. King. These units were followed a day or two later by the Oklahoma infantry, commanded by Lieutenant Colonel Elta H. Jayne, who had taken command of this organization when its former colonel, Roy H. Hoffman, had been promoted to be a brigadier general. This had occurred just before the Oklahoma troops departed from Fort Sill. Later the Oklahoma cavalry under the command of Major Donald R. Bonfoey arrived, as did the Oklahoma field hospital company, commanded by Major Floyd J. Bolend. This completed the mobilization of the Oklahomans.

The day following the arrival of the Oklahoma infantry the Texas troops began to come in. These were the newly organized units, the older organizations being sent up from the border more than a month later. After the recruiting drive the Texas infantry regiments had been formed into two brigades of three regiments each with the Seventh regiment surplus. The First Texas Infantry Brigade was commanded by Brigadier General Henry Hutchings, and was made up of the Second Texas Infantry under Colonel B. F. Delameter, the third Texas Infantry under Colonel George P. Rains, and the Fourth Texas Infantry under Colonel Charles W. Nimon. The Second Brigade was commanded by Brigadier General John A. Hulen and was composed of the First Texas Infantry, under Colonel Oscar C. Guessaz, the Fifth Texas Infantry under Colonel John S. Hoover, and the Sixth Texas Infantry under Colonel Jules E. Muchert. The Seventh Texas Infantry was commanded by Colonel Alfred W. Bloor, the only one of all the colonels to remain in command of a regiment throughout the war. Brigadier General Hulen also retained his command throughout the war, being one of the few brigadier generals of the National Guard to meet with such success.

The problems that faced the division commander upon the arrival of the troops in Camp Bowie, were staggering in their proportions. To clothe and equip the men, to organize the staff, to determine the courses of administration, and to bring about discipline in the ranks of the raw recruits were only a few of the most difficult tasks to be accomplished. Although warehouses had been constructed there was little or no clothing for issue when the troops arrived. After weeks of waiting, during which many of the recruits became barefoot and wore into rags their civilian clothes, a small quantity of summer uniforms and shoes was received but not sufficient to properly equip the entire command and the middle of the winter had passed before everyone had the required amount of serviceable clothing. Before this could be accomplished a supply department had to be organized on a large scale. The greatest difficulty however was in the procurement of supplies. Although large warehouses had been built they were empty when the troops arrived and many requisitions, were sent in before they began to fill up with the required articles.

None but the organizations which had served along the Mexican border was equipped with rifles and all organizations had to be equipped with the new pack and field equipment. The artillery had no guns, the field signal battalion no apparatus, the engineers no implements and other organizations were equally handicapped. The old pack equipment of the troops that had been in service, was out of date and unwieldy.

Like all National Guard camps the men lived in pyramidal tents calculated to hold eight men comfortably. These tents were not provided with floors and stoves until after the cold weather had set in and were not provided with lights until later. The mess halls, bath houses, stables and offices were wooden structures, although the mess halls were without floors. This condition finally was overcome after many months of hard labor but not until an epidemic of influenza had crowded the hospital to its capacity and many deaths had resulted. Fire added to the handicap of the medical corps by destroying two of the hospital buildings in the fall and another fire burned one of the warehouses. Weeks were required to reconstruct the burned buildings. Many of the residents of the camp vicinity offered to take patients from the hospital into their homes but this did not become necessary.

Indians Digging Trenches at Camp Bowie.

Among the other articles which were not supplied in sufficient quantities, were blankets and comforters. Through the agency of the Red Cross Society comforters were collected from all the larger cities of Texas and shipped to the camp to be distributed where they assisted materially in making the personnel of the camp comfortable. Tents also were lacking and for a short time there was an average of twelve men to a tent. During the period of influenza more tents arrived and the crowded condition was relieved. During the early winter stoves and hot water plants were installed in the bath houses.

Immediately after the troops began to arrive the problem of consolidating units to form larger units and additional units as prescribed in the tables of organization, published by the war department, was taken up but it was not until after the old Texas infantry regiments had arrived from the border that reorganization was actually begun. This was accomplished October 15, although organizations as grouped together did not completely adjust themselves to the new conditions until weeks afterward. In this consolidation headquarters troops for the division were made up from a troop of Texas cavalry. The 131st Machine Gun Battalion was composed of the machine gun companies from the First Oklahoma Infantry, the Third Texas Infantry and the Fourth Texas Infantry. The Seventy-first Infantry Brigade was made up of the 141st Infantry, (a consolidation of the First and Second Texas Infantry), the 142d Infantry, (a consolidation of the First Oklahoma and the Seventh Texas Infantry), and the 132d Machine Gun Battalion comprised four machine gun companies with the machine gun company of the First Texas Infantry as a nucleus. The Seventy-second Infantry Brigade was composed of the 143d Infantry (the Third and Fifth Texas Infantry), the 144th Infantry (the Fourth and Sixth Texas Infantry) and the 133d Machine Gun Battalion was formed of four companies with the machine gun company of the First Texas Cavalry as a nucleus. The Sixty-first Field Artillery Brigade was composed of the 111th Trench Mortar Battery (formed from one troop of the Texas Cavalry), the 131st Field Artillery (made up for the most part from the Second Texas Artillery), the 132d Field Artillery, made up of dismounted Texas Cavalry and surplus artillerymen, and the 133d Field Artillery, composed of the First Texas Artillery. The 111th Engineers were formed from the combined Oklahoma and Texas Engineer Battalions. The First Texas Field Signal Battalion was enlarged to become the 111th Field Signal Battalion. The 111th Train Headquarters and Military Police were formed from the similar Texas organization reinforced by recruits from all organizations in camp. The 111th Ammunition Train was made up of the First Squadron of Oklahoma Cavalry, which formed the horse section, and suitable men from all arms of the division to form the motorized section. The 111th Supply train was formed of men drawn from all parts of the division. The 111th Sanitary Train, containing the 141st, 142d, 143d and 144th Field Hospital Companies, and the 141st, 142d, 143d and 144th Ambulance Companies, was formed from elements of the First and Second Texas Ambulance Companies. First and Second Field Hospital Companies, and the First Oklahoma Field Hospital Company, strengthened by recruits from all organizations in the division. The 111th Engineer Train, formed from Officers and men taken from the 111th Engineers, completed the organizations of the division.

This was not accomplished without considerable ill feeling. By the consolidation Brigadier General Hoffman was left without a command in the division. A depot brigade was formed and he was placed at its head but later he was ordered away and did not return. Old organizations as well as new had hoped to retain their identity and serve under the officers by whom they had been enlisted. Many surplus captains found themselves without companies and were bitter in the extreme after having wasted months of their time in the vain hope of taking their companies to France. These were attached to consolidated companies for a short time and then were transferred to other camps or separated from the service. To add to this bitterness about 200 reserve officers from the training camp at Fort Sheridan, were distributed throughout the division to assist in the instruction di the troops. Most of these however were sent to other camps before many months, only those who accepted National Guard commissions remaining with the division.

Street Scene, Camp Bowie, in the winter of 1917-1918.

Before they received their uniforms and while they were still armed with clubs when on guard duty, the troops began to learn their first lessons in drill and discipline. The last was not as easy as the first. Men who had lived all their lives in. the open and managed their own affairs found it difficult to obey someone else in nearly everything they did, especially as it was not always explained why the thing was to be done. However, willingness and cheerfulness accomplished this discipline in the end and it may be said that no division in the army could boast of a better personnel than that of the Thirty-sixth. Its men were from many races. Indians from Oklahoma, Mexicans from the border country, German, Irish, Italian and Swedish settlers in the central parts of Texas, mingled with men whose parentage had been American so long they had forgotten all other, and worked shoulder to shoulder. Later they were seen in France by the Commander in Chief of the

American Expeditionary Forces, who exclaimed: "These men can go anywhere!"

The Indians from Oklahoma presented one of the most difficult problems. The division had more Indians in its personnel than any other division in the American army and at first most of these were placed in one regiment, the 142d. In this regiment a complete Indian company was formed, containing fourteen tribes. Only a few whites were in the company. One of these, a mechanic, was an Irishman, while one of the cooks was a German. Later the Indians were scattered somewhat by transfer but the company retained its identity as the Indian company until the division was demobilized.

Practice on the target range, for machine gunners and automatic riflemen, as well as for troops armed with the rifle, was taken up in the fall of 1917, even before many of the soldiers had been armed with the rifle. The Springfield was the weapon used at first but in December, 1917, a shipment of 7,000 new United States Army rifles. Model 1917, arrived and then the troops were instructed in the use of these. Enough of the new rifles to equip the entire division did not arrive until March, 1918, however, and at first the older men had great difficulty in adjusting themselves to the larger and more unwieldy weapon after having used the 1903 model for so many years. In the course of several months, however, every man m the division had fired some kind of a course on the target range and had become familiar with the new arm.

Automatic riflemen and machine gunners were handicapped to a considerably greater extent in their practice. Instead of having the new Browning models of these weapons they practiced with the French Cauchat automatic rifle and several different makes of machine gun, including the Lewis gun, the Vickers, the Colt and the Hotchkiss. About this time Major General Greble, who had been in France with Colonel Williams, chief-of-staff, returned to the division and began training the command in the methods expected to be employed in Europe.

In the fall of 1917, officers and enlisted men from the French and British armies had arrived at Camp Bowie to establish schools for the instruction of officers and non-commissioned officers in warfare as developed during the first two years of the war. They established schools in machine gunnery, the use of the automatic rifle, bayonet and grenade, the firing of mortars and defense against gas. Also a school of military intelligence was conducted and the intelligence section in all units was organized. So efficient was the gas school that every officer and enlisted man in the division passed through the divisional gas chamber sometime during the winter and spring and learned how to manipulate the new gas mask that had been fashioned for the American troops. In other schools excellent progress also was made. Each regiment and similar organization in the division soon had its own instructors in the use of the bayonet, grenade, and Stokes mortars. Bayonet courts were constructed for the practical application of this art. The bayonets were driven into the bodies of dummies, and grenades were hurled into trenches specially constructed to bring into play the maximum skill on the part of the students in the course.

While the schools were developing specialists and the range was improving the ability of the men to shoot, discipline was being instilled into officers and men alike on the drill ground and, as the first rudiments of training were grasped the more advanced work of maneuvering military bodies in the tactics of attack and defense were taken up. At first the training was entirely in the hands of the officers of the various regiments, but later the French officers in particular, gave their assistance in the instruction of tactics. This training during the winter months was hampered to a considerable extent by the heavy snows that covered the camp at various times and rendered the ground too soft for practical field work for weeks afterward. Long marches took the place of drills at such times, the men being taught road discipline as well as being hardened to long marches. Later in the spring these marches took the troops to Lake Worth, an artificial body of water about ten miles distant. On these occasions various situations were assumed to cause the troops to function as nearly as possible under battle conditions.

Bayonet practice in snow at Camp Bowie.

A short time after the reorganization of the division in the fall, the commanding general accompanied by his chief of staff and an aide de camp, had gone to Europe to get actual experience with the troops in the trenches. In December he returned and immediately efforts were redoubled to complete an elaborate system of trenches which had been started near the Fort Worth-Benbrook road soon after the camp was established. This was a reproduction of actual trenches in Europe. Wide bands of barbed wire entanglements were stretched in front of the trench system and deep dugouts were constructed. As soon as possible the troops were sent to this trench system to live for four days at a time, during which combat problems were worked out both for day and night operations. Helmets and gas masks were worn and patrols covered "no man's land" both day and night. The telephones and buzzer systems of communication were actually in operation and barrage fire of artillery was represented for the troops to follow in attack and raiding formations.

In addition to their use for this training the trenches were used to demonstrate the effect of trench mortar fire, the front line of trenches being the target. During one of these demonstrations, May 8, 1918, one of the mortar shells exploded prematurely while in the mortar, killing the officer in charge of the gun crews as well as ten of the enlisted men in the immediate vicinity. All of these were members of the gun crew with the exception of one. The accident was witnessed by approximately 10,000 officers and men and the division got its first impression of bloodshed under battle conditions.

In spite of the disadvantages under which the troops labored they made excellent progress. The appearance of the division personnel attracted favorable comment from various sources and particular pride was aroused through the fact that the Thirty-sixth was the only National Guard division in the army to be allowed to conduct one of the third officers' training camps. Excellent results were obtained from this, the graduates from the school being about sixty percent of the number originally enrolled. So successful was the school that a fourth officers' training camp was established in May, 1918, but this had to be moved elsewhere when the division finally received orders to go to the port of embarkation.

During the spring of 1918 all of the regimental commanders were sent to a school at Fort Sam Houston, Texas, for a period of six weeks and the field officers remaining at the camp were given special instruction under the direction of the British and French officers. Other officers that had been found lacking in the proper qualities had been transferred to other camps or had been dismissed from the service and constant changes in the officer personnel was another difficulty that had to be surmounted. In addition to this the division was being called upon continually for soldiers skilled in mechanical trades. These were sent to other camps over the country to do special work while some were sent to Europe to fill the gaps that had been created there or to take up newly required tasks brought about by the expansion of the Expeditionary Forces. To fill the places of these men, approximately 4,000 drafted men were added to the division in the spring and every effort was necessary to bring these up to a high point of efficiency.

Several officers from the regular army were added to the personnel at division headquarters during the last part of the winter and the first of spring, at which time a considerable number of promotions was made in all grades of the commissioned personnel. At first there had been a keen feeling of resentment on the part of many National Guard officers against the officers from the regulars but this gradually wore away.

Several times the entire division was reviewed by the division commander and in the spring the troops were marched in review through the streets of Fort Worth for the governors of Texas and Oklahoma. This occurred April 11. Thousands of people from all parts of both states filled the streets and specially constructed stands. The appearance of the animals and transportation in the trains as well as the general appearance of the men as they passed in review was the cause of many compliments and high hopes were aroused once more that the division soon would be called upon to fight.

Company "B" 142d Infantry at Camp Bowie.

The troops had hardly started to settle down in camp in the fall of 1917 before they were fixing the date for departure overseas. All of the estimates were for a date not later than Christmas and many officers as well as enlisted men made wagers on the subject. As the months passed and no orders were received many of the men grew restless and some actually transferred to casual detachments to be used as replacements for the divisions in France. During this time excellent service was rendered at the camp by various welfare associations. These provided reading rooms and social entertainment for the enlisted men and during the influenza epidemic ably assisted in caring for the sick.

In the latter part of May, confidential instructions were issued to all officers, covering the movement of the division to the port of embarkation. Every detail was considered. Only the actual date of departure was withheld. At this time the trench warfare training was abandoned for maneuvers by battalions in open warfare giving an indication of what was expected to develop in Europe. Finally in June the actual order for departure was received and published confidentially to the command, railway transportation was concentrated at Fort Worth and all surplus property was turned in preparatory to the departure.

Bayonet practice at Camp Bowie.

Chapter Two - From Camp Bowie to Brest and Redon

Preceding the division in its departure for the port of embarkation the advance party, composed of fourteen officers and as many enlisted men, left Camp Bowie July 3, and arrived at Camp Mills, Long Island, four days later, where they prepared to continue their journey overseas. It was the duty of this party to go ahead of the division to the ports of embarkation in the United States and debarkation in Europe, for the purpose of preparing the way for the coming of the main body of troops. Its duties also embraced the preparation of the training area for the troops after they arrived overseas.

The advance school detachment consisting of more than 100 men and officers, left Camp Bowie the day following the advance party, with intention of proceeding to France to enter schools, where they would be given instruction in the latest methods employed at the front. When this school party arrived at Camp Mills, however, the custom of sending advance school detachments ahead of divisions going abroad, had been discontinued. The school detachment then remained for the main body of troops and the personnel of the party sailed with the respective organizations represented in it.

In the physical examination and classification of men and officers before the departure from Camp Bowie, all who were found to be physically unfit were placed in a development battalion which was to remain at the camp. Major General Greble, camp commander, who had been demoted to a brigadier general late in February, but who had remained in command of the division, was left at the camp also in command of the development battalion and other troops that remained.

The first of the units of the division to depart, were the infantry brigades, the additional machine gun battalion and the field signal battalion. The first trains to leave the camp departed July 8, and others followed in rapid succession, the artillery and ammunition train being the last to get under way. These left Camp Bowie, July 12, and the last units had arrived at the ports of embarkation July 22. All organizations of division went to Camp Mills with the exception of the 143d Infantry, which embarked at Newport News. Virginia. Practically all railroads were made available for the troop trains. Some made their way to New York by following the general outline of the Gulf and Atlantic coasts while at least one of the trains went far enough north to pass through a portion of Canada. The greatest secrecy was practiced in covering the time of departure of the trains as well as their itinerary in order to prevent all possibility of wrecks suspected to have been planned by agents of the German government. The trip to the port consumed on an average of four days for each train. Only one accident marred the trip. One train was wrecked near Shreveport, Louisiana, one man being killed and several others injured.

Indian recruits just arrived at Camp Bowie.

At Camp Mills, command of the division passed to Major General William R. Smith, who had just been promoted from a brigadier general in the Thirty-seventh Division, where he had commanded the Sixty-second Field Artillery Brigade. Formal command of the Thirty-sixth was taken over by General

Smith, July 13, and he remained at the head of the division until its return to the United States. General Smith was a graduate of the military academy at West Point and had a recognized standing in the regular army before the war, having been in the artillery arm of the service. At the time he assumed command of the division, the Sixty-first Artillery Brigade passed to the command of Brigadier General John E. Stephens, also of the coast artillery. Brigadier General Blakely was relieved of his command in the artillery brigade a short time before the movement began from Camp Bowie.

"The Sam Browne Belt and How to Wear It" might have been the subject of many a lecture attended by one and conducted in the secrecy of the individual officers' tents after the Thirty-sixth arrived at Camp Mills. This was one of the first important self-assigned duties attended to by the officers after they reached camp. Some amusing sales were made to the over-zealous. Some of the officers were persuaded to purchase great, long belts that were sufficient to encompass their bodies twice, by the statement that it would be necessary to wear the belt over the overcoat in France. In the same manner many useless articles were sold by the enterprising vendors of officers' equipment, who had established small stores in the vicinity of the camp.

Rivalling the Sam Browne belt in its importance was the new overseas cap which was to take the place of the campaign hat. Officers and men shared in the task of adjusting this new contrivance to their persons. A remarkable variety of ideas were developed as to just how the cap should be placed on the head, many attempting to wear it after the fashion of a "stocking cap" while others gave an excellent impersonation of Napoleon. These new articles of apparel however were not allowed to be worn in New York, where men and officers went as often as time and money allowed.

The privilege of seeing New York was not given to all however. Some of the units arriving at the camp August 14, were equipped and sent aboard the transports at Hoboken the same day, not being allowed to spend a night in the camp, so great was the necessity for loading the ships preparatory to departure. In this short space of time passenger lists had to be compiled and the numerous regulations of the camp regarding physical examinations, had to be complied with. Not all of the troops were equipped with the new overseas cap, some of them being compelled to await their arrival at the training area in France before they received this part of their equipment. Other units of the division remained at Camp Mills more than two weeks, the artillery being the last to ship. One of the regiments, the 141st Infantry, had the misfortune to be sent aboard a transport that was found to be defective, and the entire command was returned to Camp Mills to await another boat. This caused a delay of only a couple of days however. One battalion of the 112d Infantry also was delayed because its transport had been found to have a bad rudder.

While the troops were at Camp Mills they underwent daily inspections as to physical fitness as well as to ascertain whether their equipment was complete. Inspectors declared some of the companies to be the best in appearance of any that had passed through the port, and the morale of the entire division was at a high point. Each lighter of troops that made its way from the ferry landing at Brooklyn to the piers at Hoboken, was crowded with the cheerful faces of men who seemed somewhat more than delighted at the prospect of soon entering upon the great adventure of their lives.

Practically all of the troops sailing from Hoboken crossed the Atlantic over a southerly course that took them far down into the Gulf Stream and in the vicinity of the Azores. The 143d Infantry, sailing from Newport News, however, went by way of Halifax, Canada, and then crossed the northern part of the ocean to Liverpool, England. Passing through England, this regiment landed at La Havre. The advance party also took the route through England, and landing at the same port in France July 22, after crossing the English Channel. For the greater part of the division the crossing of the ocean was without excitement other than that attending the first experience at sea and the novelty of strange sights. Constant boat drills were held on all the transports and every precaution taken to guard against attacks by submarines. Only the convoy of eight transports which sailed from New York harbor the night of July 31 was the exception to this rule.

Brig. Gen. Hoffman addressing troops at Camp Bowie during Second Liberty Doan Drive.

Convoyed by the United States cruiser "Charleston," these ships, carrying the artillery brigade, the ammunition train and the First Battalion of the 142d Infantry, as well as parts of other units of the division, was attacked three times by submarines and the latter part of the voyage has been declared to have been the most adventurous experienced by any convoy crossing the Atlantic during the entire war. The most serious of these attacks occurred the day before the transports arrived at Brest, France. Without warning the submarines appeared in the center of the fleet, which was guarded at the time by a flotilla of destroyers,, the "Charleston" having turned back to the United States a short time previous. The appearance of the undersea craft was the signal for every available piece of naval artillery to open fire. It was stated that more ammunition was used by the naval gun crews in this voyage than by all the other ships of the navy during the war up to that time. The guns, however, had not been able to get into action before the submarine had launched a torpedo which barely missed the stern of the "Maui," the transport bearing the First Battalion of the 142d Infantry, probably the closest call experienced by any of the troops.

Hardly had the periscope of the enemy craft been sighted than one of the destroyers was bearing down upon it, and although the submarine submerged before the destroyer reached the spot, it was not in time to escape. A depth bomb which made the sides of the transports in the vicinity groan from the shock of the explosion, ended the career of the German boat. As soon as the bomb had exploded the destroyer wheeled in her course and sped back to the spot to drop a second depth charge. In answer to this second explosion the surface of the sea in that vicinity was covered with oil and debris from the destroyer's prey.

This engagement was watched with the same keen zest known to the football field. Every available vantage spot aboard the transports was crowded with troops who cheered and cheered again as the gun crews fired their pieces and the destroyers darted here and there to drop their bombs. When the oil and debris appeared on the surface of the water the cheering was that attending a touchdown. It is thought that the convoy was attacked by the same submarines which sank the "San Juan" off Fire Island the morning of July 29, although there was no way of verifying this. In the engagements with the U-boats no damage was inflicted to the transports and the entire convoy arrived safely in Brest Harbor, the morning of August 12, being the last of the division to reach France.

In spite of the excitement that prevailed in the battle with the submarines the infantrymen aboard the "Maui" learned to display strategy that was worthy of the best. For many days it had been difficult to get enough to eat, due to the over-crowded condition of the boat. The ship's galley was not capable of feeding so many men. When the greater part of the personnel rushed on deck, the hungry doughboys found their way below and obtained a supply of provisions from the unguarded galley that left the larder practically exhausted. Another incident that later caused general amusement was brought about when all transports put on full steam to get away from the vicinity of the submarine as soon as possible. The convoy was a slow one, taking fourteen days to cross, and the troops blamed the speed on the rearmost ship, an Italian steamer, which common rumor declared to be the slow boat and the one which the rest of the ships had to wait for. When the submarines appeared, this ship developed speed that astonished those who were watching. She sped through the balance of the convoy and was lost to sight within a short time. Later it developed that the Italian boat was laden with explosives to such an extent that had she been hit by a torpedo it would have been disastrous to any other ships in her vicinity.

Not all the troops of the Thirty-sixth debarked at Brest. The sanitary units as well as some others landed at Bordeaux and St. Nazaire. However the greater number went ashore at Brest and had cause long afterward to remember their hardships there. After long days and nights in crowded ship holds where the air was bad and where they could not get sufficient exercise, the four miles between the docks at Brest and the rest camp seemed like twenty. Many of the men were so weakened that they were unable to march more than half a mile up the steep slope toward the camp before they were compelled to fall out and rest. The rest camp was a camp only in name. It consisted of open fields in the vicinity of Pontanezean Barracks, constructed by Napoleon I. These fields were covered with manure and were wholly without sanitary necessities. The only baths to be had were at the old Barracks and were not adequate, although for those who were able to get under them, they proved a blessed relief. While most of the troops were at the camp there was a constant downpour of rain although during the first two weeks of August it was declared that the weather was more pleasant than at any time during the year. The only shelter available was the shelter tents the men carried in their packs. At night it frequently was cold in addition to the dampness and one death was reported from exposure.

In spite of these hardships the troops found many things to interest them. Pontanezean Barracks was one of the places to draw the greatest attention. Many of the relics of the day when Napoleon's troops had lived there, still were in evidence. One of these was the guillotine then in use. The Barracks were of stone and were inclosed by a high stone wall, for the purpose of defense. In this enclosure the First Battalion of the 142d Infantry passed in review before President Poincaire of France, who visited the camp at that time.

As soon as they could do so most of the soldiers began their efforts to master the French language. They were startled when they marched through the streets of Brest to hear the French children sing "Hail Hail, The Gang's All Here," and very quickly they learned to understand what "Oo la la!" meant, when spoken by the demoiselles along the way. Much disgust was expressed at the mud fences surrounding the tiny fields as well as at the lack of automobiles and sanitation. Apparently nowhere were there facilities for bathing. Not far from the camp were several chateaux which were inspected with the greatest interest. The strange garb of the priests as well as the peasants and their combination houses wherein the stock as well as the family found residence, were the subject of every letter written home, and the use of the antiquated flail by the peasants in threshing their grain was so astounding that many of the troops declared the land to be not worth fighting for.

At Brest the soldiers obtained their first view of German prisoners of war. These were employed in the handling of cargoes at the docks and looked so well-fed that the Americans found room to envy them after the long ocean experience. Also they saw in Brest the first moat and walled defenses that characterize so many European cities. Although the moat was dry and a tiny street car ran along its bottom in places, yet it visualized things that had been read about in all the literature of Europe. Men, women and children were wearing wooden shoes everywhere, leather footwear being the exception. Later the "sabots" were the most common thing to be seen but to the newly arrived Americans they were wonders of another world. Every house was of stone, no wooden structures being visible.

General view of 142d Infantry tents, Camp Bowie.

French cafes located near the camp came in for their full share of attention. These were allowed by the regulations to sell light wines to the troops during certain hours of the day but were forbidden to sell cognac. In spite of these regulations however it was not difficult to obtain any and all varieties of drinks in the evening. Some of the officers as well as the men attempted to sample all of the known varieties in one evening with disastrous results. One of these, from the commissioned personnel, arrived home in the late hours of evening and discovered that his tent mate had become so disgusted with the lack of sanitation that he had posted certain signs to remind himself of home. The late arrival became so wrought up over one of these that he immediately repaired to an adjoining tent where he put his arms around the neck of a brother officer and sobbed his grief into the other's ear: "What do you think of that blankety-blanked tent mate of mine? He's put up a sign which says, 'Don't spit on the floor!'"

Practically all of the units were required to remain at Brest an average of six or seven days before trains could take them away to the training area. The destination of the Thirty-sixth Division was known as the Thirteenth training area, and was located in the district of Aube, about 100 miles east of Paris. The principal town in the area was Bar-sur-Aube, about forty miles slightly south of east from the city of Troyes. Here division headquarters was established while the various units, other than the artillery brigade, were scattered through the smaller towns in the area. The Seventy-first Infantry Brigade had its headquarters at Bligny, eleven kilometers south of Bar-sur-Aube, while the Seventy-second Brigade headquarters was placed in Soulaines, about the same distance to the north of Bar-sur-Aube. The engineers and other units were nearer division headquarters.

Part of the troops en route to Bar-sur-Aube from Brest passed through the environs of Paris and Versailles, but there was no opportunity to see the wonders of those places. Other units were sent over a more southerly route which enabled them to see such old cities as Orleans, Tour and Dijon. These latter organizations found their impressions of France greatly improved after the filth at the Brest camp. Wonderful vistas of cultivated country, where the farms were laid out in patchwork of beautiful colors, met the gaze of the travel-weary troops as the train wound in and out of the hills of central France.

Indian sentinel on duty in Camp Bowie trenches.

Fatigued with the trip on the train, as well as the experiences at Brest and on the ocean, most of the units were exhausted when they reached their training area and the march from Bar-sur-Aube to the various billets was the hardest that they had been called upon to make. The town lies in the valley of the little Aube river and is only approached from the north and south by means of two long and unusually steep hills. Up these two slopes the doughboys of the two infantry brigades were compelled to toil as soon as they unloaded from the stock cars in which they had made the journey from the port of debarkation. These were the "40 hommes, 8 cheveaux," or "A. E. F. Pullmans." made famous by the wit of the American soldier.

At Brest the Sixty-first Artillery Brigade was separated from the division, never to rejoin it. The personnel remained at Brest until August 20, when the troops were taken by rail to Redon, France. The 131st and 132d Field Artillery were billeted in Redon proper as was the headquarters, Supply Company and Headquarters company of the 133d Field Artillery, but the Second and Third Battalions of the 133d were billeted in Nicholas de Redon. and the First Battalion in Avasac, both places only a short distance from Redon. The 111th Ammunition Train, less Companies C and D, also were billeted near Redon, and remained with the artillery throughout. Companies C and D had been sent with the infantry of the division to Bar-sur-Aube.

At Redon the artillery was taken in hand by officers from the French army to begin its final preparation for service at the front. The brigade remained at Redon only until September 3, when it proceeded by marching overland, to Camp de Coetquidan, the famous French artillery training center which had been established by Napoleon I. and which was the first school of its kind in the world. Two days later the brigade began a course of eight weeks instruction which it did not complete. At the end of six weeks it was declared ready for service and was ordered to rejoin the division, then in the front lines. Due to delay on account of an insufficient number of draft animals for the light artillery, and tractors for the heavy pieces, it did not get started before the armistice was signed, November 11. The tractors which were to have been allotted to the heavy artillery were lost when the ship bringing them from the United States was sunk off the French coast. After the armistice the order sending the artillery to the front was cancelled. Thus the Artillery was not enabled to get into the fighting zone, much to the chagrin of its officers and men who had made an excellent record in their training.

Chapter Three - Training in France

Following their arrival in the Thirteenth training area the officers and soldiers of the Thirty-sixth were given a couple of days in which to settle themselves in billets, to locate ground for maneuvering, drill and target practice, and rest after the wearisome journey from the United States. Immediately division headquarters was established in Bar-sur-Aube, reorganization along the lines prescribed by the American Expeditionary Forces was demanded. In addition to the chief of staff it was necessary to have three assistant chiefs of staff and other subordinates in order to handle the movements that would be demanded of the division in the field. The three assistants to the chief of staff were known as G-1, G-2 and G-3. The first of these handled all administrative matters, such as transportation, supplies and subsistence The duties of G-2 were to get intelligence of the enemy and prevent intelligence or information being sent to the enemy. The third officer was in charge of all training and operations of the division. In this manner the handling of the division was systematized in a way then unknown in the United States. When the division left Camp Bowie it left a considerable number of its clerks and stenographers there with the former division commander, to take care of the camp, and correspondingly was handicapped as soon as it arrived in Europe.

All tents folded at Camp Bowie.

Besides the necessary changes at division headquarters there were many other shifts in the units of the division. The first task taken up by the new division staff was to eliminate officers regarded as unfit for service in the battle lines. Within a short space of time forty-five officers, including Brigadier General Hutchings, commanding the Seventy-first Infantry Brigade, two colonels, two lieutenant colonels, five majors, eighteen captains and thirteen first lieutenants and four second lieutenants were sent to Blois, France, for reclassification or discharge. Also the division lost sixty-eight other officers for various reasons, some of them being sent to school and others being transferred. To help fill these vacancies in the ranks of the officers, ninety-eight new officers were received, among them Brigadier General Pegram Whitworth, who took command of the Seventy-first Infantry Brigade. From these officers it was necessary to obtain two new regimental commanders, a division quartermaster, a division ordnance officer, a division machine gun officer and other specially trained officers. At this time an order was received making it impossible for certain positions on the staff to be filled by officers of the regular army. Consequently field officers from the regiments had to be transferred to headquarters and vice versa.

Not waiting for the new officers to adjust themselves to their tasks or become acquainted with the personnel of their commands, the division was plunged into an intensive training period that was expected to overcome some of the handicaps the men were facing. At Camp Bowie morale and discipline had been built up to a high degree. The men were healthy and willing, although sometimes awkward in appearance, especially in matters connected with strict military etiquette. Beyond the belief that they could whip the whole German army, their discipline, their willingness to do, their ability to shoot and use the bayonet, and their knowledge of conditions connected with trench warfare they were not ready to enter the field.

Only a few weeks before they departed from Camp Bowie they had been equipped with the Browning machine gun and automatic rifle and some of the units had never seen this weapon. The first task that faced the platoon and company commanders was to master the weapon themselves and see that it was taught to the men who were to use it. Another task was the instruction of the men in the handling of live grenades. They had handled dummy grenades in Texas for many months but not until they arrived in Europe did they use one that would explode when thrown. Also the knowledge of how to maneuver and fight in the open was limited and a system of liaison had to be developed from its very foundation. At no time in their training had the infantrymen advanced under the cover of actual artillery fire and this was not possible in the Thirteenth training area because of the absence of artillery to train with. Neither had a machine gun barrage ever been attempted. March discipline was another thing that had not been developed in Texas, because the division had never made long moves by marching. Many of the officers who had just been promoted were unfamiliar with their work and had to learn by actual experience.

To overcome these deficiencies many marches in which the strictest discipline was observed and daily maneuvers were the principal features of the training program. Problems for all units from squads to the division were worked out. On the target ranges the men were taken through maneuvers which called for them to fire real ammunition while advancing from one position of cover to another. In this manner the enlisted personnel obtained their best idea of what actual battle conditions would be. In all of these exercises, especially where the regiment or larger organizations were participating, the greatest stress was laid on the writing of messages and the ability of the junior officers to estimate situations. Special schools where officers and non-commissioned officers were taught the art of writing clear messages were conducted in some of the units and general progress was noted.

In the midst of this training the division was called upon to supply a large portion of its most seasoned personnel to fill the gaps in other divisions that had been fighting at the front. Eighty officers and approximately the same number of non-commissioned officers were sent away to schools to obtain special instruction in the handling of various weapons. To assist in filling the vacancies among the officers about seventy-five recently commissioned officers from the candidate school at Langres came to the division as instructors. Practically all of these were retained with the division permanently and went into action with it later. Most of these men had been at the front and rendered great assistance in training the troops in the handling of the automatic weapons.

Coulommes, where 141st Infantry located headquarters.

The failure to conduct proper liaison between units large and small and the difficulty in getting the proper kind of information from the assaulting troops were the greatest difficulties to be overcome in the training. In the short time allotted these defects were only partially overcome. The maps provided for the maneuvers were inadequate and there were not sufficient instructors but at every exercise and maneuver the greatest stress was placed on proper liaison and its importance was brought home to everyone.

Although supplied with a certain number of automatic rifles and machine guns, the equipment of the division was by no means complete, because it did not exist in Europe. Practically all available shipping had been used to transport troops with the result that the amount of supplies for these was insufficient. No Very pistols, for the firing of rockets, had ever been seen by the greater part of the personnel, and the ability to use other means of signaling was limited. Nothing was left undone to overcome these difficulties however and at no time was there a lack of confidence. Many of the units developed excellent ability to maneuver; to advance, taking advantage of every possible cover and to flank positions rather than take them by direct frontal attack. In the 142d Infantry a model platoon of the very best men available, was developed to demonstrate the manner in which the assault should be conducted against one or more machine gun nests. This demonstration was conducted for the benefit of several organizations with excellent effect. All efforts to obtain a sufficient amount of motor transportation and horses to haul the wagons and carts, already issued the division, were without result, these supplies not being in existence. Food was not always of the best or of the greatest variety. Lack of transportation caused this to a certain degree while another cause was the fact that the troops fighting at the front were supplied even when it was necessary to stint other units in the training areas.

Immediately upon their arrival in the little villages where they were billeted the troops began to make friends with the French peasants, with whom they lived, and in this manner obtained many little favors that made life more endurable. Often their billets were uncomfortable. The men frequently slept in the lofts of barns and in other undesirable places where there were no heating arrangements and where they could not keep clean. But they shared the food of the French people and spent their money freely. They learned to jabber a little French and get what recreation they could in the evening by attempting to tell the natives about the wonders of America. Training went forward under any and all weather conditions and the little time they could get in the homes of the natives proved the greatest redeeming feature of the period.

Influenza again attacked the ranks of the division during the month of August but only a few organizations were seriously hampered. The disease was in a milder form than that which was raging in the United States and the number of deaths was comparatively small. It was necessary to move some of the troops into better quarters but the schedule of training was not interfered with. Some of the infantry regiments tired an entire course of instruction on the rifle ranges. From early morning to late at night the officers and men were engaged in various tasks connected with their training and the period was filled with almost as much discomfort and hardship as was to be found at the front.

The strength of the division was still further depleted by the departure of the 111th Engineers, September 10. These troops were transferred to the First American Army Corps as corps engineers and remained with that command throughout the fighting. This brought the strength of the division down to 15,590 enlisted men and 656 officers, a shortage of approximately five percent in officers and twenty percent in enlisted men. Without the artillery, ammunition train and engineers the division should have had about 20,000 men and officers.

Although under great handicaps in some respects the division was fortunate in others. It was the first division to be armed with the Browning automatic rifles and machine guns. All other troops, including the regular army divisions had gone into the fighting zone armed with the Chauchat automatic rifle and the Hotchkiss machine gun. This had necessitated additional work in bringing up ammunition. With the Browning weapons the same ammunition that was used for the rifles of the infantry was used also for the machine guns and the automatic rifle. The personnel of every unit was hardy and accustomed to making the best of every condition. Most of the men had lived in the open and the hardships attending campaigning without shelter did not lessen m any degree their ardor to get into the fight and the belief that they were superior to any similar unit in the German army. Although the officers and men had known each other at home in the United States the discipline was not marred by this. In nearly every case the troops were loyal to the greatest degree to their officers, the most of whom by this time had come to the division from organizations other than the National Guard units from which the division originally had been formed.

French children and Medical Corps man.

During the entire training period the troops were without Stokes mortars, of which a certain number was assigned to every regiment of infantry as well as the mortar battery attached to the artillery. Neither did the infantry have tanks to train with in their maneuvers and knew next to nothing about the use of these in the field.

Considering these things the ability of the troops to take care of the most difficult situations later on, may be looked upon as all the more remarkable. Other divisions, especially the first divisions to reach France had been given many months of training before they went into the battle line to occupy a quiet sector. These divisions had been trained with artillery as well as tanks, and had been given detailed instruction in advancing by the aid of a machine gun barrage, the guns actually firing for their benefit. The Thirty-sixth had none of these things and instead of going into a quiet sector to become acquainted with the enemy under advantageous conditions, was entered in battle under the worst possible surroundings and facing the most stubborn kind of resistance. One of the regular army divisions which landed in France almost simultaneously with the Thirty-sixth, was sent to a quiet sector to the east of the St. Mihiel salient, and remained there throughout the conflict. The men from Texas and Oklahoma were sent to drive their bayonets forward through the desperate resistance of the German army, fighting with its back to the wall, and fiercely contesting every inch of ground to save itself from disaster. But the division was ready. It had been in training only a little more than four weeks but it was ready and the hearts of the men beat high at the prospect.

Chapter Four - To the Front

Orders taking the Thirty-sixth Division from the Thirteenth training area were so brief that even the division headquarters was unaware just how close to the line the command was destined to go. The order merely stated that the movement would be by rail to a new area. Prior to the receipt of this order, the division commander had been directed to send three officers to the Belfort front to make a preliminary inspection of that sector, with the supposed view that the division would be moved there for its first operation. This however developed only into a ruse for the purpose of deceiving the enemy. False field orders, maps and details of an attack, were left purposely where they might be picked up by enemy agents. These false plans promptly disappeared and within a short time five enemy divisions were moved to that point to make a defense against the supposed attack, while the First American Army was hammering its way forward in the great drive between the Meuse River and the Argonne Forest.

The orders sending the division from the Thirteenth area were received at headquarters in Bar-sur-Aube, September 23, and two days later the actual movement of the troops began. First all salvage was collected and disposed of. A great amount of extra equipment that had been issued at Camp Mills before the troops sailed from the United States, was discarded because it could not be carried in the field. The small amount of transportation in the division was not adequate to gather up all the salvage and much of this was left in the little towns where the troops were billeted, to be collected later by the salvage organization of the army. Grenades and other explosives were buried in places where they could do little or no damage and much privately owned equipment, that had been carried up to that time was presented to the French peasants. A few companies carried all their blankets many miles to the trains, while others employed French carts to transport this part of their equipment.

Chateau de Flogery, headquarters 71st Infantry Brigade near Tonnerre, France.

Although in the area but a short time the soldiers and the peasants had formed strong attachments. Many of the older women, who had lost relatives in the war, wept as the troops marched out of the little villages and everywhere the natives lined the roads to wish the soldiers a "bon chance" (good luck). Entraining points were at Bar-sur-Aube, Bar-sur-Seine and Brienne le Chateau, and although some of the units found it necessary to march many miles over hills to the railway stations, the march was conducted in an excellent manner. The troops were placed on the trains in good order and all sections began the movement promptly. This was done in spite of the fact that machine gun carts had to be hauled to the railroads by hand, there being no animals to draw them. In one instance it was necessary for an organization to march sixteen miles, although the march table had been prepared with a view to cause the minimum amount of marching to all units.

The day the Thirty-sixth left the area around Bar-sur-Aube, the grand assault of the First American Army between the Meuse and the Aisne Rivers was launched. The St. Mihiel salient had been reduced earlier in September and in the month previous the line between Reims and Soissons had been straightened, until the Marne salient had been eliminated. This had followed the assault of the First and Second American Divisions operating with the First Moroccan Division (French Foreign Legion) south of Soissons. At the same time the First American Army was fighting its way forward in the operation of the Meuse-Argonne, the Fourth French Army under General Gourard was forcing the Germans out of their Hindenburg defenses in the Champagne. This was between Reims and the Aisne river, or just to the west of the First American Army. The First American Army had as its aim the capture of

Sedan and the severing of the German forces, while the Fourth French Army was working in the direction of Mezieres, another important railroad center just to the west of Sedan. To the east of the Fourth French Army was the Fifth French Army, the two being under the general command of General Retain. The drive that was being conducted by all of these combined forces in reality was that which had been expected to develop in the spring of 1919. The tendency of the German forces to retire however called for the advance to be made at this time and strategy demanded that every available combat unit be hurled against the crumbling enemy defenses, in order to hasten their collapse and bring about a hasty end to the struggle. For this and only this reason was the Thirty-sixth Division called upon to perform a herculean task, although unequipped and without experience under fire.

It was to move into the area occupied by the Fifth French Army that the division left Bar-sur-Aube, although this information was not received until the first elements were ready to go aboard the trains. The Thirty-sixth and the Second Divisions had been placed at the disposal of the French high command, the Second Division being assigned to the sector of the Fourth French Army. Later it became known that the Thirty-sixth was expected to be used in a follow up movement should the French develop strength sufficient to break the German line east of Reims. Had this been the case the Americans would have been used to push forward vigorously after the line was broken and to exploit the ground beyond. At the time the Texas-Oklahoma division was sent to the Fifth Army, large bodies of cavalry were massed in the same vicinity with the hope that they might be able to operate successfully should the German line collapse.

Headquarters 142d Infantry, Vaux-Champagne.

Epernay, second only to Reims in the production of champagne, was designated as one of the detraining points for the division in the new area, and Avize, a village a short distance southeast of Epernay was the other. Both of these places were about thirty miles almost due east of Chateau-Thierry and directly south of Reims, At Avize the headquarters of the French Group of Armies of the Center was established but in spite of this the French officials apparently were not expecting the troops of the Thirty-sixth when they arrived there in the middle of the night. The trip from Bar-sur-Aube had been only about eighty miles in length but more than five hours had been consumed in travel. At the detraining places the troops unloaded in pitch darkness, lights of any kind being prohibited. The advance parties that had been detailed to precede the division had been unable to reach their destinations ahead of the first troop trains because they did not know where the destinations were to be. In a drizzle of rain that came down steadily officers as well as soldiers found shelter, side by side, wherever shelter of any sort was available. The ruins of the abandoned railway stations served to protect some while others sought refuge in other ruined houses in the towns, that had been bombed repeatedly by German aircraft. When the dawn came it revealed the first destruction that the men of the Thirty-sixth had witnessed. This was the first time the troops had approached near enough to the fighting zone to see the effect of bombs and frequently during the night they had hushed their conversation to listen to the artillery fire just to the north of them. Some of those who had been unable to find a place to sleep had gone to the edge of the towns to see the flashes of the big guns, which at times were faintly visible.

The motor transportation of the division had been sent overland from the Thirteenth training area but the troops did not wait for the arrival of this. As soon as they were able to see their way about they began preparations for breakfast. Ingenious cooks were able to prepare coffee and some hot food and immediately afterward the troops fell into ranks and marched away to the north. The roads were heavy with mud and the marching was difficult in the extreme. The men were cramped with cold and attempts to sleep in uncomfortable places but the sound of the guns, that were to be heard more plainly with every mile traversed, served as an incentive to keep up the spirits of all.

No preparations had been made in this area to billet the American troops but each unit was assigned certain villages and, although these were insufficient to care for all, the best was made of the condition. Due to the lack of transportation the problem of bringing up subsistence and other stores from the railways was the greatest. In this work all of the motor transportation was employed and the French furnished some relief with a small number of wagons. In this area the machine gun battalions received a few mules for their machine gun carts. Rolling kitchens and water carts for all units were promised but were not received. The division had to rely on its field ranges, which were not enough for the number of men who had to be fed and were difficult to move from one point to another. Only one water cart to a regiment was issued and this did not begin to supply the demands of the troops. In the matter of ordnance the division was more fortunate. All the necessary trench mortars were supplied by the French as well as grenades and other munitions. In the moves, however, the grenades were lost by the division's service of supply and were not available until too late. The French also supplied the division with all the necessary equipment for firing signal rockets, as well as spare parts for the mortars and 37 millimeter guns.

All units of the division were billeted in the area by September 29, three days after the departure from Bar-sur-Aube, division headquarters being located at Pocancy, a little less than ten miles to the west of Chalons-sur-Marne. In the various towns around Pocancy the balance of the division was concentrated. It was in this area that the troops gained their first knowledge of how it feels to be under the enemy's bombing squadrons. Both Chalons-sur-Marne and Epernay were bombed by the Germans two nights after the division entered the area. The greater part of the personnel was located in billets about half way between these two places and the explosion of the giant missiles caused the earth to tremble throughout the intervening territory. Up overhead the steady roar of the avions' motors brought a sound of possible menace to the soldiers on the ground below, but in spite of this every officer and man was outside the billets straining their eyes to pierce the darkness and get a possible glimpse of the enemy planes. Some of the men appeared with their rifles to take a shot and no one seemed to think of seeking cover. The destruction wrought by the bombs was frightful. Six houses in a row in Chalons were reduced to fine pieces of debris by half that number of bombs. Several women and children were wounded, as were some French soldiers billeted in Epernay. Following the raid the French avions were heard going over the enemy's lines all through the night and the following day reports were circulated that a dozen towns occupied by the German troops had been bombed in retaliation for the enemy's attack.

While in this part of France the soldiers heard many stories about the first battle of the Marne, when the Huns had been turned back in their first effort to seize Paris. At Avize they were told how the French infantry in their red breeches had charged the German machine guns with no weapons but their bayonets, having exhausted all their ammunition, and how the Huns had been forced to flee for their lives. The Pocancy area lies just to the south of the river. In the little villages the Hun cavalry had paused to feed on the chickens and other food to be procured from the farmers. While preparing to sit down to such a meal in a farm house near Champigneul the German horsemen had been so surprised by the rapid advance of the French that they abandoned their chickens and rabbits on the table, where they had just been placed for them. The poilus ate the feast that the Uhlans had prepared and then pressed on to the north to push the enemy back over the river.

"The Marne has been a very good river to France," a French aviator explained earnestly. "It has been a good river to us twice. Each time it stopped the Hun when for him to have advanced would have meant disaster for us. Yes it is a very good river."

Following the air raids on Chalons and Epernay the men were more careful about displaying lights in their billets at night and about smoke appearing during the day.

At Pocancy the division was joined by Special Service Unit No. 586, one of the ambulance organizations from the United States that had been serving with the French for many months, and which had twenty-four Ford ambulances that later were of the greatest assistance in handling the wounded.

The G-2 section of the division experienced the greatest difficulty in getting a sufficient quantity of maps of the area. Only small maps that gave little information of the country were available and these were insufficient in number to be of any service to the units that needed them most. The map making machinery allowed for all divisional organizations, was not furnished. Perhaps from this more than from any other reason the division was handicapped in its future operations. Accurate maps of the country and more definite information would have saved many lives in the first engagements. But the morale of the men apparently was not affected by these shortages. Everywhere they remained cheerful under the most trying circumstances and made the best of everything. While grave anxiety was causing those at division headquarters many sleepless hours and the division commander was seeking in vain to get supplies from G. H. Q., the troops were going calmly about their training. This had to be carried on in the sheltered places where they could not be observed by the German aircraft. Under the trees the individual soldiers carried on in their various tasks, supremely confident of their ability to beat the enemy no matter how short the supplies might be.

To take care of any sickness or injuries that might develop in the area two of the field hospital companies set up their hospitals immediately upon arrival but only a few patients were received. In spite of the cold and damp and the extremely poor quarters in which most of the men were housed, the personnel remained healthy. Billeted in shacks that had been occupied by the native troops from Africa as well as labor troops composed mostly of coolies from the East Indies, the men yet remained remarkably free from vermin and most of them managed to bathe at least once in a while in the area. Part of the good health may be attributed to the fact that canteens operated by English women afforded several of the towns a place for writing letters, reading and refreshments. A great number of letters were written each day, every man making an effort to describe to the people at home what his surroundings were and the impressions made by the artillery fire.

When the general assault by the French Armies had been launched against the Hindenburg line in the Champagne late in September, they had succeeded in breaking through that defense in practically all places where the assault was made, but they had been unable to force the Germans any great distance beyond. The defense had been especially stubborn to the northeast of Chalons-sur-Marne, in the vicinity of what was known as Blanc Mont. This was a high ridge due north of the town of Suippes and at whose southern base lay the ruins of the town of Somme-Py. Here two assaults of the French had failed. Then the Second American Division, composed of the Ninth and Twenty-third Infantry, forming the Third Brigade, and the Fifth and Sixth Marines, forming the Fourth Brigade, as well as the Twelfth, Fifteenth and Seventeenth Field Artillery, and other units, had been called upon to take the heights. The Americans succeeded so well that the Germans were caught in their observation towers on the ridge before they were aware that the attacking troops were upon them. But beyond the hill the Marines especially came under such heavy fire that they were obliged to halt and consolidate their positions as best they could. Their ranks were terribly depleted and it was not considered possible for them to advance further, if indeed they could hold their ground in the face of a serious counterattack. In this delicate situation a hurry call was sent to the Thirty-sixth for one brigade to fill in the gap, by forming a second line of supporting troops behind the Fourth Brigade. For this purpose the entire division was transferred to the Fourth French Army under General Gourard and the Seventy-first Brigade was ordered to proceed to the relief of the Marines.

Camions or French trucks to take the relieving troops in two relays, arrived in the Pocancy area the afternoon of October 4, and the 142d Infantry as well as the 132d Machire Gun Battalion was directed to proceed in the first relay to Suippes and Somme-Suippe, where they would rest until the other troops in the brigade were brought up. This night will be recalled as one of the greatest discomfort to all members of the brigade. In the early evening the soldiers loaded into the camions which set out in the dark, without the aid of lights. At this time the men were equipped with only one blanket each. The night air was cold in the extreme. The movement of the camions, or trucks, made it colder. Jolting made it impossible for their passengers to sleep. The best that could be done was to huddle together for the sake of warmth and hope that the destination would be reached as soon as possible. Passing through Chalons, the grotesque figures of the military police appeared in the gloom to give the drivers directions. The camions halted just long enough for these instructions and then sped on into the night. Cigarettes were barred. The lights from these might reveal the movement to the enemy.

Finally, about two hours before the dawn the last of the camions in the first convoy arrived in the ruins of Suippes. Those who had been asleep in the bottoms of the trucks were aroused from their slumber and all unloaded, to march to their camp about two miles further to the east nearer the village of Somme-Suippe, while the camions retraced their way to the area west of Chalons, to pick up the 141st Infantry. It was several hours after dawn when the latter arrived and found places in the half-dugouts, half-shacks that had been allotted to the brigade for the resting places during the day. Still without rolling kitchens, the cooks set up the field ranges and prepared coffee and warm food. Many of the men were so hungry they could not sleep. Breakfast over, the only order issued was obeyed immediately, every fellow went to bed and obtained as much rest as possible.

Brigade as well as regimental headquarters tor both regiments of infantry were established in the town of Somme-Suippe, where later the dump for baggage for the entire division was located. In and about the town also were numerous French and French colonial troops as well as military police from the Second Division. Here the men of the Thirty-sixth learned to recognize tanks for the first time, some of the small models being parked in the town under camouflage awaiting a time when they were to be used. Here the roll of the artillery at the front was continuous and all through the day the airplanes of the enemy as well as the Allies could be seen circling in the air while the shells from the anti-aircraft guns dotted the sky with tiny puffs of smoke when they exploded. An observation balloon floating lazily behind the Allied lines proved keenly interesting, especially with so many of the enemy planes in view.

In fact so many interesting things were taking place that most of the troops preferred to sleep only a short time during the morning. In the afternoon they were paid for their lack of rest when a large batch of German prisoners were brought back from the front lines where they had been captured a few hours before. There were both old and young men among these and for the most part appeared to be in a bad plight. They were dirty and unkempt in appearance, none having shaved for several days. Their clothing was ragged and hunger was expressed in every face. All were herded into a pen surrounded by barbed wire where they were to remain until sent further to the rear. Several of the men attempted to talk to the "krouts," in the German tongue, only to be astounded when some of the prisoners replied in very good English and explained that they had been in the United States. Some had lived for many years in America and most of them appeared to be rather glad that they had been captured.

The strength of the brigade at the time it arrived in the Suippes and Somme-Suippe area was 247 officers and 5,955 men. The authorized strength for the brigade was 267 officers and 8,211 men, as provided for in the tables of organization. Attached to the brigade at this time was a detachment of the 111th Field Signal Battalion, consisting of one officer and fifty-five men. Both the infantry regiments as well as the machine gun battalion were short a great number of draft animals and wagons. The 141st Infantry by this time had received two rolling kitchens. These were all that were in the brigade. Partly because they did not realize the extent of this handicap, partly because they could not have been discouraged under any conditions, the troops were in fine spirit. The field signal detachment was better equipped than the others in everything but transportation, and efforts were not being spared at division headquarters to get equipment to the brigade before it entered the line. Officers were sent to Chalons and other places to procure additional means of transporting water and rations. The next day these efforts were partially successful in that some water casks were hauled to the command posts of the regiments actually in the front line and later rolling kitchens enough for the whole brigade were received.

During the afternoon of October 5, Brigadier General Whitworth, who had been instructed that his brigade would be employed with the Marine brigade, reported to the commander of the Second Division, Major General John A. Lejeune, whose post of command was located on the road from Suippes to Somme-Py, about a mile north of Souain, or three miles south of Somme-Py, At that time the Second Division had not received instructions that the brigade from the Thirty-sixth was to operate with it. After a short conference, in which the general situation was discussed. General Whitworth and his adjutant returned to their headquarters in Suippes to await further instructions.

These instructions arrived about 8 o'clock in the evening following the conference. General Lejeune summoned General Whitworth and his unit commanders, Colonel William E. Jackson, commanding the 141st Infantry, Colonel Alfred W. Bloor, 142d Infantry, and Major Preston A. Weathered, 132d Machine Gun Battalion, for another conference. This word reached the machine gun commander too late to attend but the general and his two colonels reported to the command post of the Second Division, where they received orders that the brigade had been placed in the twenty-first French Army Corps, and that it would relieve the front line of the Second Division the night of October 6. This was received with considerable surprise, as former instructions had been to the effect that the brigade would only take over from the Marines, or half of the front occupied by the Second Division. The instructions received from General Lejeune were that the entire front line of the Second Division would be relieved. This was the beginning of misunderstandings which later cost the relieving troops heavy losses.

Sunday morning, October 6, orders were issued to all units of the brigade to get under way for the front. All company and other organization property, as well as personal belongings of the officers, that would not be of actual service in battle, was placed in the regimental dumps at Somme-Suippe. Field ranges were abandoned since they could not be carried into the lines and set up there, and all extra subsistence supplies were stored to be salvaged. The troops fell into columns and all units were on the march before 7 o'clock. By this time most of the men realized that they were marching into actual battle. This was the time of trial that all had been looking toward ever since they first donned the uniform more than a year before. In the marches of previous days they had always felt that there was no particular reason why they should not fall out if their strength failed. But this was a different kind of march. To fall out on the way to the battle line was disgrace, and although it was to be the hardest test of strength and endurance that they ever were destined to face, there was to be no straggling as long as will power remained.

Retracing their steps to Somme-Suippe, and then to Suippes, the columns turned due north in their march and deserted the highway. The main road from Suippes to the north was literally filled with all kinds of traffic on wheels. Here was a field artillery piece, being dragged along by men as well as by horses when the occasion demanded. Behind it would be a string of combat wagons filled with all kinds of supplies for the fighting men. Then would be a water cart, a camion laden with water casks and trucks filled with ammunition and supplies for the various branches of service. These were all going toward the front. On the other side of the road would be a countercurrent of ambulances carrying wounded, empty trucks and wagons going to the rear for more supplies, and here and there on both sides of the road would be a wrecked wagon or other vehicle, broken in the press of getting to and from the lines. In this jam of traffic there was no room for the doughboy. Before the column had proceeded more than a kilometer from Suippes it was necessary to march by the side of the road.

Command Post of 142d Infantry, October 8.

Before two kilometers had been placed behind them the marching troops found themselves crossing the lines of defense which had been occupied by the French through more than four years of fighting. A little farther to the north, in the vicinity of Souain, of which scarcely a vestige remained, the former German defenses were encountered. No more desolate scene existed in all the western front, than existed here. For miles on every side there was no vegetation. The entire face of the earth was covered with debris. Mines had added their fury to the exploding shells, upheaving the ground in all directions. Trees had been shot away until they were only jagged stumps sticking out of the mangled soil. This is the "naked land" of France, the "Champagne pouilleuse." Since the beginning it has refused the efforts of those who have tried to cultivate it. The pine trees represent the first victory over the land which formerly was entirely barren. First the resinous trees and then late the wiry grass. Nothing else has been produced there simply because the soil refuses to give it life except here and there where the tiny streams connect the scattered villages.

Formerly this had been a land of beauty, of inhabited places where the grass furnished grazing and where the planted pine groves not only relieved the barren appearance but added a freshness to the scenery that was highly attractive. The whole Champagne country is a great knoll of heavy chalk. Along its rivers, the Seine, the Aube, the Marne, the Velse and the Aisne it had presented graceful outlines that were lovely in the extreme. From the great knoll tiny streams had run in every direction to empty into the larger rivers. The Suippe is the largest of these tributary streams and into it empty the Ain and the Py, while the Tourbe, the Bionne, the Dormoise and the Alin empty directly into the Aisne. At the source of each of these little streams formerly was a village, or in the language of the country a "Somme." As the result of this the villages have been called Somme-Tourbe, Somme-Suippe. Somme-Bionne and Somme-Py. Sometimes the "somme" was shortened into "sou" thus developing the name Souain,

This was the scene of the most terrible struggles between the French and the German armies in September and October, 1915, or just two years before the men of the Thirty-sixth marched across it. Here the grandest offensive conducted by the French during the entire war took place. On a front more than twenty-five miles in width they drove into the German lines and tried to break through to hurl the invaders out of the land. Failing, they settled down to a stubborn defense that made raids of nightly occurrence. Sometimes the lines would be raided by both sides twice in one night. Here the bursting shells had set fire to the houses of interlaced logs and thatched roofs with such readiness that scarcely one of these remained. Constant exposure to fire had left hardly an undemolished stone in Souain. Of the giant mill that formerly was located there nothing but a bit of the wheel remained. Churches that had stood through six centuries were crushed to powder by the high explosive shells of both sides and the splendid highways that had been main arteries of travel since the days the first Roman road builders entered the country, were torn and shattered by shells until in places they ceased to exist.

The Champagne pouilleuse has always been historic ground. Frederick the Great in his campaigns met his first serious reverses in this country around Valmy, and before that time through all the history of France the battles in the Champagne had been most numerous. The highway of the Romans from Lyon to the English Channel had passed through this country. In 1915, the French cavalry had practically its only opportunity to fight in this locality. At a critical moment in the fighting two squadrons of Huzzars had the boldness to go to the assistance of the French infantry, which was attacking Allonge wood, and to assault sword in hand, the German defenses. In the fight more than 600 Germans were captured.

Here the country also lent itself admirably to the construction of deep galleries and shelters. The chalk made sleek sides for the trenches and retained its form readily. It did not wash in the rain, thus being easy to keep up. In their defenses the German officers were especially comfortable. Their dugouts elaborated year after year until they were not only safe but comfortable in all kinds of weather. In one was found a piano and billiard table, while many were well furnished with large beds and upholstered chairs. In one was found some women's garments.

But the country as witnessed by the marching doughboys in 1918, had lost all its former attractiveness. Unable to follow the road on account of the congestion of traffic, they made their way in and out among the barbed wire entanglements and maze of trenches which had been occupied but a short time before by the opposing forces. Thickly scattered through all parts of the former lines were "dud" shells of all calibers. Some of these were almost as large as a man and all were avoided carefully. They had been known to explode with but a slight jar after remaining in exposed positions. Here and there were the graves of both French and German dead. In that part of the field which had been "no man's land" for a long time, these graves were particularly noticeable, the dead having been buried in the night where they had fallen. The marching of necessity was slow. It was in the afternoon before the columns approached the vicinity of Somme-Py and for the first time came within the zone of fire.

Boche strong point south of St. Etienne, the morning of the attack.

Through the greater part of the previous night the regimental commanders with Brigadier General Whitworth had been in conference with Major General Lejeune concerning the details of the relief. The plan outlined by the commander of the Second Division provided that during the morning and afternoon of October 6, the troops would be assembled in the valley of the Py, near Somme-Py, and would wait there until nightfall before attempting to relieve the lines of the Second Division. The shortage of transportation, ordnance equipment and other supplies in the Thirty-sixth Division, was pointed out to the commander of the Second Division and he provided for his supply train to haul the ammunition, machine gun carts and machine guns to a point near Somme-Py from where they could be taken into the lines by the troops that were to handle them. In addition it was directed that the Second Division would establish a dump near Somme-Py, that it would furnish the Seventy-first Brigade with a certain number of water carts, a million rounds of rifle ammunition and a sufficient amount of signal pyrotechnics and grenades. Due to the fact that the brigade had no animals to haul its one-pounders and mortars from. Suippes, it was agreed that these weapons in use by the Second Division would be turned over to the relieving troops. Another conference was held the afternoon of October 6, at which time a roll of maps was handed to each regimental commander but it was found later that the front lines had not been traced on these and that they contained little or no information. The maps had to be pieced together, which required so much time that they were not completed soon enough for the use to which they were to be put. At this conference the details of the relief were gone over. The relief was to start immediately after dark and was to be completed by 3 o'clock the following morning. Guides were to be furnished from the front line organizations and were to meet the relieving troops at Somme-Py.

When the Second Division had attacked the Germans at this point in the line they had gained the heights of Blanc Mont with ease but when they pressed forward along the northern slopes of the hill, they met such heavy resistance from the enemy that they were compelled to halt and dig in. Some of the assaulting troops made places for themselves in shell holes while others dug small fox holes and some utilized a portion of German trenches apparently constructed for training purposes. Blanc Mont is a range about 250 feet high running generally east and west, for seven or eight kilometers, and having its highest point about four kilometers northwest from Somme-Py. Its northern slopes form half of the water shed for the Arnes, a small tributary of the Suippe. About 4 kilometers from the summit of the hill and located on the little stream is the village of St. Etienne-a-Arnes, before which the Marines had been halted and north of which was rising ground on which the Germans had planted their artillery and machine guns in such fashion as to observe and sweep every foot of the ground north of Blanc Mont. This had been the cause of heavy casualties among the units of the Second Division. On these slopes the enemy had constructed some intrenchments and arranged a defense of barbed wire, which while not elaborate, was well placed for the purpose.

A line running generally north and south through the village of St. Etienne marked the western boundary of the Second Division sector, as well as the western boundary of the Twenty-first French Corps. West of this line was the Eleventh French Corps whose right element was the Seventh French Infantry. From this line the sector of the Second Division extended about four kilometers to the east and the advanced positions of the Marines and Third Brigade were generally about halfway down the slope from the top of the hill to the village of St. Etienne, which had been entered but not held by the assaulting troops. The right elements of the Second Division, the Ninth and Twenty-third Infantry, were to be relieved by the 141st Infantry, while the left elements, the Fifth and Sixth Marines, were to be relieved by the 142d Infantry. Both the regular army brigades had been organized into provisional battalions. Two of these provisional organizations held the first line, two others were placed in the support positions while the reserve line was held by a third pair.

Before the actual relief was begun each regimental commander designated the distribution of his troops as follows: In the 141st Infantry the First Battalion was ordered into the forward position, the Second Battalion into the support position and the Third Battalion into the reserve line. In the 142d Infantry the Second Battalion was placed in front, the First Battalion in support and the Third Battalion in reserve. Companies of the 132d Machine Gun Battalion were given to each regiment. The 141st Infantry was to establish headquarters in the command post of the Ninth Infantry, while the 142d Infantry was to take over the headquarters of the Sixth Marines. Two days rations, water and ammunition were to be supplied the relieving troops at the dumps, in Somme-Py. The ammunition was distributed as were the rations but on account of the constant shelling by the enemy's guns little water was obtained. Also the blanket rolls of the men were dumped at this point, nothing being carried to the front lines other than the lightest equipment.

When the guides from the Second Division arrived at Somme-Py in the afternoon the shelling in the town was so heavy that they immediately took shelter and did not make their appearance until about 8 o'clock. All of these guides had been brought back to Somme-Py in trucks and were not as familiar with the roads as was necessary. In addition to this handicap, some of them were not found in time to guide the relieving elements. Others who were to report to the 142d Infantry reported to the 141st Infantry instead, and vice versa. Resulting from this most of the elements of both regiments were led astray. Before some of them had been gone from the village an hour they were completely lost. The guides and troops then retraced their steps to Somme-Py and began all over again. Some of the elements repeated this performance a third time before they finally emerged on the right road.

The beginning of the movement out of Somme-Py was marked by a heavy increase in the number of shells being hurled at the village by the long range enemy guns. When they arrived south of the village earlier in the day the troops came under fire from the enemy for the first time. With nothing less than awe the men had watched the bursting of the gigantic missiles loosed from the enemy artillery. With widened eyes they watched furtively for the flash and smoke accompanying the bursting of each shell, sometimes as far as a mile away, sometimes near at hand. Each burst shook the ground for a great distance in every direction and each made a hole in the earth that would have harbored a small delivery wagon or a half-platoon of men. But all of the shells did not burst. Now and then the senses of the soldiers would be drawn taut at the screaming approach of one of the great missiles, but instead of the crash of the explosion with its blinding flash and deafening roar, there would be only the thud of steel against mud. These invariably elicited the expression: "Another friend of the United States in the German munition factories."

This shelling was directed for the most part on the roads and as it increased in the early evening the wandering troops frequently found it necessary to break up into detachments and hug the places of shelter to avoid casualties. This could not but result in confusion. Some of the troops became separated from their commands in this manner and only were located and directed properly after hours of effort. By this time it had been discovered at headquarters that something had gone wrong. Staff officers were sent hurriedly out on all roads regardless of shell craters over which their motorcycles were operated. The confusion gradually was overcome and all units headed in the proper direction.

No one can describe properly the misery of this march. Few thought of making complaint. If a man chose to swear it was done under his breath. All realized that the hardship was a matter of necessity and all demonstrated a training discipline that would have been a credit to any troops. They stuck to the task and "carried on" as long as strength lasted. A few did fall out. In each instance the man would stagger onward until the help of his comrades on either side and the determination to stick it out would avail no longer. But these were few. They had been tired with the march of the morning and because of the excitement of being under fire, the necessity of securing rations and ammunition and of disposing of their packs, not many had obtained any sleep during the afternoon. There had been no straggling during the day and there was none in the night. Men and officers who fell by the side of the road were evacuated to the hospitals but pride kept the others going. Many a man would have given up in the early hours of the night had they been in any other place. But going into battle, each gritted his teeth a little harder, and although the straps of even the light combat packs numbed his shoulders, although the rub of a stiff boot heel was like the scorch of a branding iron, although his knees wobbled a bit under his weight, continued to struggle on through the darkness, laughing at the futile blasts of exploding shells, which shook the earth and rumbled their detonations of intended death.

Now and then one of these would make a direct hit on this or that roadway and one of them took away two men of the 142d Infantry. These were the only casualties. Although warm enough for comfort while marching, each halt left the ranks shivering from the night air. Midnight came but brought little rest. At stated intervals the columns would be allowed to take a breath. At these times men dropped in their tracks from sheer exhaustion but when the time came for them to move forward again, somehow they managed to get to their feet. As measured by the standards of the American soldier, it always has been a stain on a man's reputation to fall out on a march. Even in times of peace and training periods it had not been approved in the Thirty-sixth and now that they were going forward in the face of possible death it was not to be thought of. Rather than fall out it were better to die!

It seemed that dawn would never come. But few kept track of time. The night was divided into periods of marching and stops. Toward morning the men were so exhausted that the officers leading the columns dared not march for periods longer than thirty minutes. But at last the gray of dawn came and with it the blessed announcement that just ahead where the pine trees were dripping with the weight of fine rain the troops dug in by the side of the Second Division men they had come to relieve. In the shallow holes they excavated to secure shelter from the constant fire of the enemy artillery, they made themselves as comfortable as possible. With gravel for a bed and their equipment for a pillow most of them fell into fitful slumber, too weary to know or care how close the shells were falling. The last of the infantry line companies settled into position about 7 o'clock in the morning, but elements of the 132d Machine Gun Battalion did not arrive in position until noon. Headquarters company of the 142d Infantry did not get into position until night, it having been returned to Somme-Py after having been lost hopelessly.

In the meantime the adjutant of the Seventy-first Brigade had received three copies of a map showing the distribution of the troops in the sector and the relative positions of the enemy. But he failed to deliver these maps to the regimental commanders until the afternoon of October 7, too late to serve their full purpose. This and the fact that many of the troops did not get into position in the line until the night of the seventh were regarded as two of the main contributing factors in the losses that followed. But of these things the men in the fox holes knew nothing. Scarcely conscious of their surroundings they lay in waiting throughout the day in the drizzle that made their shelters all the more comfortable. Patiently they rested in their holes ready for the time when they would go forward to the attack.

Chapter Five - St. Etienne

The northern slopes of Blanc Mont are covered with growths of pine and underbrush which thin out as the village of St. Etienne and the Arnes are approached. Beyond the edge of these trees and underbrush the country is open and for anyone to venture out of the cover was to draw fire immediately in the day time. At night the roads and trails, all of which had been accurately plotted by the Germans during the years they had occupied the ground, were harassed by machine gun fire as well as artillery fire. When the troops of the Second Division had pressed on after they captured Blanc Mont, some of their elements had been able, by means of depressions in the ground to gain positions in advance of the points where the trees ended and the open ground began. But these positions could not be consolidated and resulted in large gaps in the front line, through which it was possible for the enemy to filter his troops under cover of darkness as well as during the morning fogs which were frequent. In this way the badly disorganized units of the assaulting forces were constantly threatened with being cut off from the rear and captured. There were not enough troops to continue the advance farther and it was impossible to consolidate the lines because the existing gaps were directly under fire from the enemy's carefully selected positions. The plight of the Second Division units was serious when the relieving troops of the Seventy-first Brigade arrived and it was soon explained why the men of the Thirty-sixth had been obliged to endure such hardship in order to avoid the possibility of having to abandon the ground that had been gained at such heavy cost. Everywhere through the trees were to be found the bodies of the German and American dead, testifying to the slaughter.

Opposing the Americans in this sector were three divisions of the enemy, the Seventeenth, the 195th and the 213th. These divisions were made up of the Eighth Jager regiment, the 149th Infantry regiment, the Eighteenth Pioneer Battalion, the 368th Infantry, the Seventy-fourth Reserve regiment, the Seventy-eighth Infantry, the Ninetieth Infantry, and the Eighty-ninth Infantry. Their strength never was accurately determined by the intelligence section but it was assured that they were much below their normal battle strength. Also their morale had been affected to a certain extent by the reverses the German armies had been meeting along all fronts since the early part of the summer. At least this was true in some of the regiments. Others, however, could not have fought better under any conditions. Also these troops apparently were supplied with sufficient food although this was of a poor quality. Their bread was black and coarse and their meat was inferior. Of munitions the enemy was supplied far beyond what could possibly be used. Through his shortage of gasoline it was impossible to move many of his field pieces and everywhere in the area there were huge stacks of ammunition. Added to this the enemy, to a man, knew every foot of the ground. They were able to lay their guns, large and small, where they would cause the greatest execution.

To a naturally defensive position the Germans had added strength by stringing barbed wire from tree to tree in the woods and placing strands of entanglements in the low places where they would serve best against troops advancing under any cover that the folds of the earth provided. Each possible opening through these positions was covered by machine guns and snipers, armed largely with the far-carrying Luger automatic pistol. These machine gun positions were arranged one in rear of the other so that no sooner would one be captured than another would open fire. With enormous stores of ammunition available and no opportunity to take it away with them in the event they were forced to retire, the German artillerymen apparently were trying to shoot it all at the Allied lines. From the time the Seventy-first Brigade entered the sector it was under a constant bombardment. Shells from German 155s and Austrian 88s, the two calibers most commonly used by the Huns, crashed among the trees throughout the day and night, the bombardment being especially violent in the early morning and late afternoon, when it reached the volume of a barrage.

The day and night of October 7 was in the nature of a day of preparation although little preparation was possible. Many of the units did not finally get into position until the night of the seventh or the early morning of the eighth. Lack of transportation made it impossible to bring up warm food to the front lines and the men were forced to eat a part of their reserve rations. The water in their canteens was exhausted and there was little opportunity to secure more, because none could be hauled from the wells at Somme-Py except in the one water cart provided for the brigade. But if they could do nothing else the men could burrow down in their shallow fox-holes and rest in spite of the constant crashing of shells in the pine groves about them. Now and then an enemy plane would appear overhead and spray the ground with bullets from machine guns before the Allied planes could come up to inter-

Church in St. Etienne. Note the steeple.

fere. The troops were so well hidden under the thick branches of the pines that little damage was done, however. Late in the evening of the seventh all the cooks in the regiments were sent to the rear to prepare a hot meal on some rolling kitchens that had been provided, but in the darkness and the confusion the meal was not prepared in time to get to the troops in the support and first lines.

During the morning of the seventh the trains of the brigade arrived from the area west of Chalons, from whence they had been marching since the day following the departure of the troops in camions. They had reached the camp near Somme-Suippe the afternoon of the sixth, and then had been ordered to the vicinity of Somme-Py by Colonel Bloor, commanding the 142d Infantry. However, the supply of rolling kitchens did not arrive and the water cart situation was not relieved. The greatest difficulty had been encountered in the march from Suippes to Somme-Py. The French Military police had insisted that the trains take the same route as the infantry, off the main road, because of the great congestion in traffic, but this had been found impossible and the commanding officer of the trains, had gone back to the highway over the protests of the police and managed to get to the lines in time to serve the troops during the engagements that followed.

P. C. of First and Third Battalions in St. Etienne. Later regimental P. C. was established here.

In the evening of the seventh, details were sent back from practically all the infantry line companies to secure supplies of hand grenades. These were the light offensive grenades of the French, It was generally understood that there was to be an attack the morning of the eighth. This had been expected from the time the troops began to enter the sector but as the day grew into night and no instructions were received by the company and battalion commanders it was thought that the plan had been abandoned. Each company and platoon commander trusted that this was true because up to that time only the smallest amount of information had been obtained of the position. No maps had been distributed to the companies and only the most general idea of the terrain was to be had. It was known that the enemy had particularly commanding positions on the right and left of the sector because during the afternoon of the seventh, messengers attempting to communicate with the Marine outpost on what was known as Hill, or elevation, 140, in the right of the 142d Infantry sector, reported that they could not reach the position because of fire from the enemy machine guns. One runner was killed attempting the passage and the others gave up the effort. During the morning of October 7, a patrol of six Germans was captured in the rear of this hill, having been enabled during the darkness and fog of the morning to filter in through the gap in front of the village of St. Etienne, At the time of their capture they were trying To return to their lines with the information they had gathered.

The evening of the seventh regimental commanders were summoned to the command post of the brigade to receive verbally from General Whitworth, the following warning order:

"71st Infantry Brigade Headquarters,
7th October, 1918—19:45 O'clock, (7:45 P. M.)

"Warning Order:

"1. This brigade will attack upon its front in the direction of Cauroy-Machault, within the lines of the sector now existing. We will be assisted in the attack by tanks and supported by the Third and Fourth Brigades, Fourth Machine Gun Battalion and the Artillery of the Second Division.

"2. We are to take and hold line as indicated on map. The scheme of action will be — positions of regiments unchanged, battalions will advance close behind the barrage with the tanks. A standing barrage will be laid down at a point to be given, which will last one half hour. Battalions will pass through the first line battalions during the standing barrage of one half hour. When the final objective is reached a standing barrage of one hour will be laid, at which time, the third line battalions will pass through to take positions, either to exploit the success or to prepare to hold the objective.

"3. Tanks assisting in the attack will aid in destroying machine gun nests. As these nests are encountered infantry will delay their attacks to allow the tanks to overcome the machine gun nests. As soon as this is accomplished the attack will continue.

"4. Outposts beyond our present line will be withdrawn at H hour minus thirty minutes. The rate of advance will be 100 meters in four minutes.

"5. Carrying parties should be immediately organized and sent to the divisional dump to secure grenades (on the basis of four hand grenades and one rifle grenade per each man) and also obtain the necessary pyrotechnics.

"6. Plan of Liaison will be that prescribed by the Second Division.

P. Whitworth,
Brigadier General."

"Delivered in Person."

This verbal order from the brigade commander was the result of orders issued from the headquarters of the Fourth French Army and the twenty-first French Army Corps in turn, for an attack which was calculated to not only capture the village of St. Etienne-a-Arnes but Machault, the next village five kilometers to the north. This was for the purpose of hurrying the withdrawal of the enemy from the vicinity of Reims, twenty-five miles to the west. To stay the assaulting troops and enable the German forces to retire in good order from the direction of Reims, it was expected that desperate resistance would be offered.

At the time they received the verbal warning order the regimental commanders were given maps showing their sectors and the objectives that were to be taken. It was after midnight, however, when the regimental commanders reached their posts of command and after 3 o'clock the morning of October 8, when all of the battalion commanders reached these headquarters for their instructions. In the meantime the regimental commanders had been sent copies of the Second Division order directing the attack and accompanying this was a chart indicating where the barrage was to fall and the points where it would be laid for prolonged periods. Before these instructions could be explained to the battalion commanders and these commanders could return to their posts, it was time for the attack to start and they were useless as far as the commanders of the combat units were concerned.

During the day of the seventh, repeatedly it had been reported from the French on the left as well as the Marines in the front line positions that they had possession of St. Etienne. Contrary information which came back to the commander of the 142d Infantry, caused that officer to request that a body of Marines be sent to occupy the village until morning to assure that the assaulting troops would be protected from that location. Sometime during the night of the seventh it was reported to Colonel Bloor that two provisional companies of Marines had occupied the town.

Preparatory to the attack Colonel Bloor had arranged for transportation to bring up the Stokes mortars and 37 Millimeter guns from the point where they had been left near Suippes. These had been distributed in the line and were for service in the attack. Conditions as to information received by both assaulting regiments were about the same. The front lines were practically parallel and it took as much time to get the information to one as to the other. Inaugurating its assault the left of the 142d Infantry line would debouch into the open with Companies E, F, G, and H, in the two assaulting waves. The right of these companies were facing a small patch of irregular pines on Hill 140, or what became known later as Barton's Hill. Practically all the front of the 141st Infantry composed of Companies A, B, C, and D, was facing similar woods, which had to be penetrated before the assaulting troops would debouch into the open for the second phase of the attack, against the heights beyond St. Etienne and the Arnes rivulet. Those company commanders who had been warned that an attack might begin the morning of October 8, waited in vain for any intimation of it the evening of the seventh. In the cold drizzle that made the atmosphere heavy and depressing and which seemed to accentuate the crash of the bursting shells in the pines, they waited as patiently as they could and prepared their commands with what instructions they could give. Several men had been wounded by the shell fire during the afternoon and evening and there was a growing restlessness to be doing something.

"Over The Top"

As the first gray of dawn began to appear through the pine tops, runners scurried here and there through the brush to all parts of the line summoning company commanders to the battalion command posts. Practically at the same time the batteries in the rear began to thunder their first barrage. It was time for the troops to be under way. Hurried instructions, all too brief, all too indefinite were flung at company commanders and these hurried back to their commands to state as briefly as possible to their platoon leaders what they had learned at the battalion command post. Before this could be accomplished it was time for the barrage to move on and for the troops to be pressing forward. Before the company commanders could get back to their commands the shells from the enemy batteries were beginning to fall thick and fast in the trees, a barrage that was intended to block off the supporting waves from the front, so that they could not assist in the advance.

In the front lines rapidly the word of instruction was passed from captains to lieutenants, and from lieutenants to non-commissioned officers and privates. In the din of the barrage bursting well beyond in the open, words of command were drowned but first one man here and there and then all rose from the places where they had burrowed in the chalky soil and moved steadily forward. Somewhat dazed by the newness of it all, uncertain as just what task they had to perform, handicapped by the lack of complete instruction, yet they never faltered. Sure and confident that they could meet and master any foe, unafraid of any death that might await them, gloriously they went forward in a manner that might do credit to the best trained troops in the world. For a few moments they were an organized whole, moving as if in practice maneuver. Then they encountered the wire. They had not been able to take full advantage of the barrage where this was properly laid. Some were a little late in starting because the word had not reached them. Picking their way through the strands of wire that had been cut here and there they were met by a perfect hail of machine gun and rifle bullets. Trained through the months for just this kind of emergency, promptly they sought cover wherever available on the ground and then took up a series of isolated fights for the capture of this or that position from which the enemy had opened fire.

Damage done by Boche shell in St. Etienne.

Ensconced behind trees before the 141st and well camouflaged in positions between the 142d and St. Etienne, in many instances the "boche" machine gunners had not come under the American barrage. This had been laid beyond them. The information that told of the occupation of the village had caused the artillery to lay their fire down beyond this. Actually between the first line troops and the village was one of the strongest positions held by the Germans. All the "boche" gunners had to do was to lay their sights and wait for the men of the Thirty-sixth to reach the wire.

The Assault of the 141st Infantry.

Short and irregular ravines, which were overgrown with scrub pine thickets and some underbrush and which afforded every opportunity for laying machine guns so that the enemy would have every advantage, featured the terrain over which the 141st Infantry was called upon to advance. The front line of this regiment followed generally the road from St. Etienne to Orfeuil being slightly north of this road at the left of the regimental sector but dropping away to the southeast until it was considerably south of the road in the center and on the right flank. It was a poorly consolidated line, large gaps existing between the positions in front of the road on the left and the positions occupied by the troops in the center.

To overcome these conditions the troops of the assaulting as well as the supporting battalion had considerable difficulty. Major Edwin G. Hutchings. commanding the First Battalion, in the assault position, assembled his company commanders a short time after midnight, the morning of October 8, and gave them detailed instructions as to the disposition of their troops in the attack. All companies were represented at this conference with the exception of Company A, whose commander on the extreme right of the sector had not been located by the runners sent to summon him to the battalion command posts. It afterward developed that one of the runners was killed in attempting to carry the message to the company and others lost their way in the darkness. Instructions were given at similar conferences held by Major Hawkins of the Second Battalion and Major Benjamin F. Wright of the Third Battalion, in the support and reserve positions respectively.

The only thing that the battalion commanders had not been able to tell their officers was the exact hour at which the barrage would commence and the assault get under way. This word was received shortly after 5 o'clock or only a few minutes before the firing began, but it was passed hurriedly to the companies in time for them to get set for the start with but little confusion. Company A was the only exception and the commander of that organization, taking his cue from the movement of the other companies, began to advance only a few moments later. A short time before the time for the assault to begin, Company B of the 132d Machine Gun Battalion, formed to accompany and support the assault echelons of the First Battalion. Company A of the 132d Machine Gun Battalion was assigned for duty to the supporting battalion and the regimental machine gun company was with the reserve.

Hardly had the drumming regularity of the American and French barrage been fairly well launched before the enemy batteries began to retaliate into the ranks of the regiment formed for the assault, as well as among the ranks of the supporting battalion several hundred yards to the rear. For the first few minutes of the advance the men of the 141st found little difficulty in making their way forward in the center but no sooner had they appeared across the St Etienne-Orfeuil road than they came under machine gun and rifle fire in such volume that they were staggered and took cover. On the left the units already across the road met instant resistance when they started to advance. The men of Company A also met early resistance on the right. In spite of the galling fire of the enemy artillery and the deadly accurate firing of the Maxims here and there small groups or individuals worked themselves forward for a short distance and closed with the enemy machine gunners. This was slow work and costly.

Having advantage of a complete knowledge of the ground as well as concealment the German snipers and machine gunners manned their guns skilfully. Those machine guns which were captured only opened the way for others to begin firing. In a short space of time all liaison between units of the assaulting companies had been broken up. Many officers had been put out of the fight by wounds and several killed. Platoons broke up into small groups and then became intermingled as the men fought for themselves.

In order to give strength to the assault Major Hutchings had placed himself at the head of Company C, after sending the company commander with a part of his force to lead the attack elsewhere. Hardly had he started forward with this company than the battalion headquarters group with the battalion commander leading came within the range of a high explosive shell. Major Hutchings was killed instantly, several of his runners were severely wounded and direction of the attack was lost completely. Here and there officers with small groups of men working forward, strengthened themselves in their positions and held on. By the most dogged kind of work they dislodged the enemy machine guns here and there but failed to drive the gunners from their vantage places farther forward, with the result that the advance was halted.

Another house in St. Etienne after the bombardment.

Troops of the supporting battalion coming up from the rear only served to make the line denser and increase the number of casualties. These men of the Second Battalion rendered able assistance in dislodging some of the Germans from their positions but they also had been thrown into confusion in starting the attack. In the excitement that followed the beginning of the barrage and the rain of enemy shells the battalion commander had lost control of the situation. This was largely through his determination to swap the positions of his two flank companies. The left company had been ordered to take position on the right and the right company to take position on the left. Later the battalion commander left the field and although some of the companies were completely confused they made their way to the line and joined the assaulting waves.

The Third Battalion also became identified with the assault battalion before the morning had grown into the afternoon. But the addition of these men to the line failed to continue the advance. Major Wright commanding the reserve battalion had been wounded severely, and was evacuated before he had time to effectively place his battalion in the line. He later died of his wounds. This left the entire regiment without majors to take charge of the various units, which in many instances were under non-commissioned officers. Some of the companies had all of their officers killed or wounded.

In this emergency Colonel Jackson, commanding the regiment, went to the line in person and directed the attack as best he could. Apparently the situation could not be improved. The advance had been slight, especially on the left and the slaughter had been terrible. In the trees and underbrush it was practically impossible to co-ordinate the many separate little groups of men for any concerted movement. With seasoned troops this condition might have righted itself but with men who were in the firing line for the first time it was a superhuman task. In some places the assaulting elements retired to their original line and remained there. Others, notably a detachment on the extreme left remained in the advanced position it had gained and held its ground despite threatened counter attacks from the enemy in the late afternoon. The automatic riflemen and machine gunners laid their weapons in such fashion that the one counter attack which developed was repelled immediately before it could hardly get started.

Some of the units coming up from the rear had wandered to the left and entered the sector of the 142d Infantry, where a few of the men became identified with the ranks of that regiment, but the greater part found their way back to the 141st during the afternoon. Toward noon the enemy repeatedly sent his airplanes over the line and obtained observation that enabled his artillery to register with deadly effect while there was no apparent effort of the Allied planes to retaliate. In addition to directing the artillery fire the "boche" airmen swooped down over the 141st lines and poured bursts of machine gun fire at the men among the trees. The number of casualties from this was not large but it served materially to halt the efforts to advance the line farther.

At the close of the day the front line continued to follow in a general way the outline of the St. Etienne-Orfeuil road. Most of the assaulting elements were north of the road but not sufficiently advanced to dislodge the machine gun positions of the enemy, which were registering on the troops advancing in the left half of the brigade sector. Two detachments of the regiment had pushed so far in advance of their supporting troops that they were threatened with being cut off but they were not in positions where they could bring their fire to bear on the marching, gunners, who were holding up the attack on the left flank. In the first darkness of the night efforts at reorganizing the line were begun and as many as possible of the positions were consolidated, or connected together. Few efforts were made to re-establish companies as originally organized, but here and there detachments were grouped into provisional organizations and placed under an officer.

The regiment had suffered heavily among the officers. Besides Majors Hutchings and Wright, five other officers had been killed outright. In the First Battalion, First Lieutenant Graham B. Luhn had fallen while leading a portion of Company D. Other officers of this battalion had been wounded severely and sent to the rear, but this was the only death.

Where Company A command post was established after the counterattack.

In the Second Battalion. First Lieutenant Clyde T. Morrison had been brought down while in the very front of the fight. He had advanced with his men well into the woods, giving a splendid example of courage, when he had been mortally wounded.

The heaviest casualties apparently were in the Third Battalion, the last to get into the assault waves but which suffered the loss of Second Lieutenants Aubrey W. Cox and L. C. Alcorn of Company K, Second Lieutenant John C. McKinney of Company L, and Second Lieutenant Joseph M. Burchill of Company M. The death of these officers, each of whom had been a platoon commander, made reorganization difficult in the extreme. At the beginning of the assault the strength of the regiment had been approximately 2,560 officers and men. Of this number seven officers and 187 enlisted men had been killed. Eighteen officers and 348 enlisted men had been wounded. Additional officers and enlisted men had been reported missing in action and gassed sufficient to bring the total casualty list to thirty officers and 607 enlisted men.

In considering the losses that occurred among the officers and men of the Seventy-first Infantry Brigade in its attack on St. Etienne-a-Arnes, it is noted with increasing interest that regiments engaging in every major operation participated in by American troops, including the assault at Cantigny, the terrible fighting in the drive south of Soissons in July, 1918, in the St. Mihiel operation and in those desperate struggles that took place in the Argonne between the Meuse and the Aisne rivers, lost only about thirty officers killed and in many of the companies lost less in killed on the battle field than was lost by many of the companies of the Seventy-first Brigade in the three days before St. Etienne.

The Attack of the 142d Infantry

Conferences and detailed plans for the advance in the sector of the 142d Infantry had been rendered impossible by the delayed arrival of the battalion commanders. These had a much longer distance to travel from the regimental command post to their own headquarters than had been the case with the 141st Infantry and Colonel Bloor had been delayed in receiving his instructions. In the Second Battalion, selected as the assault Battalion and commanded by Major William J. Morrissey, the company commanders had been summoned to assemble at the battalion command post by means of a telephone message from regimental headquarters. This message had directed that the captains be assembled by the time the battalion commander again reached his dugout. However, Major Morrissey was not able to return over the long distance from the command post of the regiment to the front line until approximately 5:20 o'clock, by which time the barrage already had been under way several minutes. The troops had received no word of an expected attack and merely waited in their positions as the friendly barrage developed and the counter barrage from the enemy's batteries began to fall m the areas behind them. Similar conditions existed in the First Battalion in the support position, commanded by Captain Charles Kuhlman, as well as in the Third Battalion, under the command of Captain A. M. Greer, and which was in the regimental reserve. In the Third Battalion however the instructions were given a few minutes after the conference at regimental headquarters, the short distance enabling Captain Greer to meet his officers immediately and to outline the plan for the assault and explain the mission of his troops. In the First Battalion the officers were summoned to the battalion command post only a minute before the first guns began to roar their defiance at the enemy. Gathering there they received a few brief words of instruction, to the effect that the attack was to be launched at 5:15 o'clock and to be conducted in a generally northern direction. All were enabled to glance at a map but none had an opportunity to study its details. They were informed that before they could return to their commands it would be time to go and they scurried away without further parley.

Under the circumstances no troops in the world could have behaved better. As soon as possible Major Morrissey had sent his company commanders back to their companies and these in turn had delivered their instructions to their subordinates. By this time the barrage had lifted from the position on which it had been falling for twenty minutes and rolled on. The most advanced positions of the Germans had been relieved from the crash of the bursting shell. Realizing this the front line company commanders waited for the one-pounder sections and the Stokes mortar platoon to send over a few shells to disconcert the enemy and then, as steadily as if at maneuvers the men rose from their places and began to move forward. By this time the enemy's shells were falling thick and fast in the entire sector. The crash of the larger shells mingling with the sharp crack of the smaller projectiles made a deafening roar. Here and there men were being hit but no one gave heed.

Where officers of 142d Infantry are buried at St. Etienne. More graves of enlisted men in background.

The assault battalion had been arranged with Companies H and G in the first wave and Companies E and F in the second wave. On the right of the sector where the troops jumped off from a position directly on top of Hill 140 they came under fire from the enemy machine guns in a strong position among the trees on the northern slope of the hill before they had advanced fifty paces. To add to their discomfort they also were caught by flank fire from the right. Taking advantage of the cover afforded by a sunken load they rushed forward in groups, that ran and fell and rose to advance again, until the men were flanking the position on two sides. In this part of the assault the captain of the leading company was among the first to fall, being hit by two machine gun bullets a short distance in front of the jumping-off position. Other officers, among them Captain David T. Hanson, Medical Corps, and First Lieutenant Richard Harrison, Company F, were killed in the first few minutes after the attack started. Captain Hanson, wearing the Red Cross insignia of his service was killed instantly while seeking to take care of some wounded men. He had gone with the very first elements of the assault far in advance of the position required of him. Lieutenant Harrison was killed immediately after his company had become merged with the leading company. The latter had been held up by a machine gun nest on the northern slope of Hill 140. These as well as other officers had been brought down before they had a fair chance to estimate the full situation and give directions. Company F, in the second wave soon became intermingled with the ranks of Company H in the first wave and the command was assumed by Captain Willis L. Pearce, in command of the second company.

In the left of the sector. Company G in the first wave and Company E in the second wave, had encountered heavy belts of wire as they advanced against the village of St. Etienne, from which no resistance had been expected. Up to the time they reached the wire they met little resistance but in climbing ov6r the low strands of entanglements and working their way through the openings here and there, these men literally were mowed down by fire from three enemy strong points, one in the cemetery to the east of the village, one in a depression directly between the advancing troops and the town, and one in a camouflaged position in the open ground to the southeast of St. Etienne. These positions were undisturbed by the fire of the barrage which had been placed beyond them. Here the assault was completely checked. Members of these companies naturally worked to the east in the vicinity of Hill 140, in their efforts to advance, and some obtained positions of vantage behind hillocks and the trunks of trees near the sunken road leading from the hill toward the town.

This was the situation when the companies of the First Battalion coming up in support behind overtook the assault and gave it impetus. In this battalion. Companies A and B were in the first wave and Companies C and D in the second wave. Starting from their positions it had been necessary for them to pass in squad columns, or single file, through the trees down the northern slope of Blanc Mont and through the barrage placed by the enemy's batteries to cut off the supporting troops from the fight. Advancing several hundred yards in this manner before they reached the jumping-off position, the men of this battalion suffered heavy casualties from shell fire and lost their commanding officer, Captain Kuhlman. The burst of a shell wounded half of the battalion headquarters group, including several runners. In this advance the men of Company D failed to follow the wake of Company B and wandered into the French sector to the left, where they remained through the balance of the day. Captain Kuhlman had been so severely wounded that it was feared for a time that he would not recover and his loss did not become known to his company commanders until the middle of the afternoon. In spite of this however the companies continued to function properly. The volume of the enemy's fire had increased as the supporting troops were seen to emerge from the woods and, as they debouched still farther into the open, the high explosive shells were mixed with gas. Resulting from this were many gas casualties later in the day, the men continuing to advance at the time, not realizing the extent of the poison in their lungs and throats.

Continuing the advance beyond the jumping-off position Company A struck the line of resistance just to the north of Hill 140, where the attack of Companies H and F had been held up, while Company B encountered the same wire that had obstructed the path of Companies E and G. Company C followed in the wake of Company A. In these companies grenades had been distributed prior to the beginning of the assault As soon as the right companies had arrived before the machine gun nest held by the Germans on the northern side of the hill, a detachment of these grenade men worked their way to positions of vantage as did a group of automatic riflemen, and a deadly concentration of fire was poured into the position. These efforts, combined with those of the other two companies, that already had flanked the position on two sides, soon brought about the reduction of the stronghold.

Graves of enlisted men of 142d Infantry who were killed before St. Etienne.

Out of their dugouts and from behind the rocks and scrub trees where they had sought refuge, more than 100 Germans with their hands above their heads, crept whimpering toward their captors. Some cried the well-known surrender cry of "kamerad" while others apparently could make no other sound than that similar to the whine of a whipped cur. Officers and men stood ready with pistols and bayonets to cut short the slightest move toward treachery. The prisoners were herded to the rear and placed in the hands of the Marines, who were holding their positions until the success of the advance could be assured. With the machine gun nest overcome the troops pushed on toward the Arnes to the east of the village.

On the left the men of Company B had encountered fire equally as severe as that which had greeted the first two companies. Unmindful of this, however, they had continued to work their way forward in the depressions of the ground. Captain Wilmot Whitney, commanding the company, was wounded but continued to advance with his men. First Lieutenant Arthur J. Matheny, second in command was killed instantly just after he had crossed the last belt of wire. A short time later Second Lieutenant Thomas F. Collins was killed by the burst of a shell and before long every officer in the company had been sent to the rear with wounds. Assisted by the men of Company B the other two companies continued to press the attack and in a short time also were helped by the troops of the Third Battalion, who had come forward to join in the assault instead of waiting in the reserve. The combined efforts of these forces and the fact that the position on the right had been overcome soon brought about the reduction of the strong points south and southeast of the village. Here more than 100 prisoners also were captured, also many machine guns and automatic pistols. But the cost had been heavy. More than thirty men in Company B had been killed and more than fifty wounded. Other companies had suffered almost as severely but they continued to press forward.

The fighting around these two positions lasted more than two hours and at the end only a few elements of the three battalions had been held out of the attack as supporting troops. Practically the entire Third Battalion was in the line as well as the First Battalion. These combined forces swept onward toward the Arnes and the outskirts of the village. In the latter phases of the attack against the positions southeast of the town, able assistance had been rendered by Companies C and D of the 132d Machine Gun Battalion. These had been assigned respectively to the assault and support battalions. These had placed their guns in position on the hill and had poured a volume of fire upon the enemy positions that rendered them untenable. As the advance then continued across the undulating ground to the east of St. Etienne and the troops came under the heavy fire from the position in the cemetery, the machine gunners again rendered able service by increasing their range and pouring a steady stream of bullets into the Hun defenses. In this and the subsequent defensive work the machine gun company of the 142d Infantry also played a conspicuous part.

All of this time the long range fire of the German machine guns on the slopes to the north of the village had been steady. Time after time these would sweep the little plain but without apparently affecting the onward rush of the assaulting troops. A machine gun placed in the steeple of the church in St. Etienne, was causing considerable damage in the ranks of the advancing battalions until a well-placed shot from one of the 37 millimeter rifles caused the German machine gunner to tumble from his perch. This machine gun had been able to cover the entire area of open ground over which the support and reserve battalions had been compelled to advance after leaving the woods in the earlier phase of the attack.

With this gun out of action and the positions in the cemetery under the direct fire of the American machine guns, the infantrymen closed in on the Germans in the graveyard. Part of the assaulting troops made their way through the edge of the village and took the Germans in the flank while others rushed the cemetery from the front. Here the struggle assumed hand-to-hand proportions before the cry of "kamerad" again sounded and additional prisoners were sent to the rear. As these prisoners passed over the plain to the east of the village the German artillery as well as the long range machine guns on the slopes to the north of the little stream and the village began, to register among the prisoners, causing heavy casualties and many deaths. Some of the prisoners were bearing wounded to the rear when they were killed by the bursts of Austrian 88s, German 77s and 155s.

In the cemetery. Company A command post was here October 10 and 11.

As they advanced across the open ground to the right of the cemetery, the attacking troops once more came under heavy barrage fire from the enemy artillery. In moving forward from the captured position on Hill 140, Captain Willis Pearce, who had been in command of the two companies around the first position, was killed. Here and there along the banks of the Arnes the men dug in and strengthened their position as best they could. Automatic rifles were placed where they could best be brought to bear on the enemy and patrols were pushed out across the creek to locate the positions of the Germans on the slopes ahead. These patrols drew such heavy fire that they contented themselves with digging in along the Arnes and waiting for the better organization of the lines. While actively engaged in this reorganization, Captain Carter C. Hanner, commanding Company E, and who had been in the front of the battle since the early morning, was fatally wounded by machine gun fire. He was carried into an abandoned German dugout and given first aid treatment but expired within a short time.

In the fighting before the village when the Third Battalion became merged with the assaulting echelons, two other officers had been listed among the killed. The first of these, First Lieutenant Alfred N. Carrigan Jr., was killed instantly while leading his company toward a position where it could take the position in a flank movement. A short time later Second Lieutenant George Goebel of Company M, was killed by a bursting shell. This completed a toll of eight officers killed before the middle of the afternoon, Companies B and H having no officers remaining to command those organizations.

The advance to the little creek had been accomplished by the early afternoon. From the time the troops reached the stream they were under an intense bombardment by the enemy. The water supply was getting low and the ammunition becoming scarce. The wounded occupied the attention of those able to dress their wounds and place them in positions where they would be sheltered from the fire as much as possible. Everyone was too busy to establish liaison to the right where the 141st Infantry had been expected to advance and nothing was known of those troops. The combat liaison platoon of the regiment had become lost in the attack and had joined the ranks of those in the assaulting waves. In the late afternoon the enemy's fire reached the proportions of a barrage and, from the sector where it was expected the 141st would be on the right, the Germans appeared in assault formation. It was a counter-attack against the right flank and came with an unexpectedness that would have staggered the most veteran troops. Here and there men turned to the rear, but others dropped coolly into shell holes and began firing their rifles

Grave of Commander of 18th Infantry Division Boche Forces, St. Etienne.

and automatic rifles. Gradually the line swept back toward Hill 140 while the left remained stationary at the village. In the gathering dusk some of the most advanced positions held by individuals here and there fell into the enemy's hands but the greater part of the ground gained in the morning remained in American hands.

Men cut off in the counter attack had many interesting things to relate about their experiences in the enemy's prison camps as well as the manner in which they were captured. One of these, Private John H. Martin, Company A, 142d Infantry, had been surrounded as he lay in a shell hole firing his rifle. His ammunition gone there was nothing to do but surrender. In telling of his experiences he said:

"I had seen one of our fellows take fifty Dutchmen to the rear and I thought maybe one 'kraut' might try to take me back toward Germany with him. I knew if that happened he would just be out of luck with all the trees scattered around. But there wasn't a chance. Another prisoner out of Company I was put with me and four Heinies started out with us. Two were in front and two behind and they had their guns pointed at us every minute.

"After we started to go back the American artillery began to put over a barrage and I am here to state that the German barrage is bad but it isn't anything compared to the ones we put over. I just about had it figured out that we weren't going to get through alive. The two Dutchmen in front took out and the two behind began to prod us with their bayonets and tell us to run, but there wasn't anything stirrin' and I told one of them if he wanted to run to take out and I would manage to get along all right."

Private Joseph Krepps of Company A, was another of the men who held their ground until they were cut off by the German counter attack. But it was not until 2 o'clock in the morning that he finally was captured. Time after time he evaded the enemy behind the German lines only to come in contact with a whole company about 2 o'clock and fall into their hands before he realized his position.

Among these men who were cut off and captured was Sergeant Norman Duff, who probably had the most interesting experiences of all the men taken in the counter attack.

"I didn't feel so bad about it when I finally got back to the German rear and found about twenty marines back there," he declared, "but when they got me that afternoon I never felt so foolish in all my life.

"I had ducked into a Dutch dugout to escape the shell fire in the barrage preceding the counter attack and when I started out they were pumping machine gun bullets against the entrance so fast I thought to myself that I was hardly fast enough on my feet to dodge all of them. Finally these let up and out I popped but no sooner than the bullets again began to scratch around for my feet and I landed in a shell hole. By that time it was getting dark and I figured I'd just lie there until a little later and then make my way back to the company.

"Well, about that time I heard several men coming from the direction of our lines and at first I wasn't just sure who they might be. Then I heard their voices and I knew they were neither Americans nor Frogs. So I just lay low in that hole and waited for them to pass. They passed all right but I guess I was too impatient. I thought they had gone but when I put up my head to take a look I was staring straight at a kraut who exclaimed, 'Ah, Amerikanner!' I didn't say anything because I was too full of thinking what a nut I'd been to look up or move at all. They were too many for me and there wasn't anything to it but to lay down my rifle like he told me and play the obedient.

"They took me back to the man who was acting as an intelligence officer and his first question after he learned my name surprised me some. 'Are you out of the One Hundred Forty-second or One Hundred Forty-first Infantry?' he says. I didn't see any use in telling a lie there so I told him the truth. But when he asked his next question I had some fun.

"'What formation are you using in attack?' he says.

"I didn't exactly know the correct answer to that one myself but I said: 'We are not using much of any certain formation in this attack but there are four other divisions behind ours getting ready to come through here behind our brigade and they are due most any minute.' As far as I knew that was true and he didn't seem to know any better himself.

"The next day they took us through the town of Attigny where we saw a lot of Russian prisoners at work digging under the bridge which they tell me was blown up later so our fellows could not chase the Dutch across the river.

"All of the Huns I talked to told me that if we would just be patient a little while they would be hiking out of France and leave it to us. That seemed to them to be a much better plan than fighting for it and causing so many men to get killed.

"They were trying to move everything toward the rear as we went back. There were hardly any horses to be seen and instead they had Jerry soldiers hitched to wagons. They did not try to make us haul any of these and they would have been out of luck if they had made the effort. One of the Jerries who had been shot through the ankle tried to keep his hand on my shoulder to help himself along but I couldn't see that at all so he remarked that I was no good.

"We were taken to Rastatt, in the 'Black Forest of Baden,' where all of the American prisoners were kept and remained there until after the armistice was signed. After we got there we were given food sent through by the American Red Cross and finally this organization took us back to France through Switzerland."

In the village the troops had placed themselves in strong positions. A detachment of Marines had assisted in establishing a line in front of the village and a detachment of Second Engineers and Marine machine gunners had been placed in the cemetery to assist in holding the line in the event of further counter-attacks. Patrols beyond the village to the north soon discovered the enemy in a strongly fortified system of trenches behind barbed wire entanglements. This system was not large but was complete and would offer strong resistance.

In the beginning of the attack tanks had been employed to assist in breaking up the enemy machine gun positions but due to the fact that the assault was late in starting and the small knowledge the infantrymen had of tank tactics these were of little value. Although the tanks advanced over the ground in the vicinity of the German positions between the assaulting troops and the village, they apparently either had not discovered these positions or were unable to dislodge them. Neither were they able to operate against the machine gun nest on the northern slope of Hill 140, where the terrain was unfavorable to tanks.

As the afternoon faded shovels were plied vigorously by both officers and men in an effort to make their positions strong enough to be defended successfully in the event of another counter attack in the morning. There was no opportunity to count the dead and wounded. Here and there an officer had gathered a detachment of men from all companies in the regiment about him and organized them as best he could.

Two of the most conspicuous acts of gallantry in the entire war were performed on the slopes of Hill 140 during the early part of the morning and brought the Congressional Medal of Honor to the two enlisted men responsible for their accomplishment. These were Corporal Harold L. Turner, Company F, 142d Infantry, and Sergeant Samuel H. Sampler, Company H, 142d Infantry. Both of these men came from the same locality in Oklahoma, Corporal Turner living at Seminole and Sergeant Sampler at Mangum. In all its wars the United States has presented but few Medals of Honor, the decoration being more difficult to attain than any ribbon given for distinguished service in action by any nation.

After his platoon had started the attack, Corporal Turner assisted in organizing a platoon, consisting of the battalion scouts, runners and a detachment of signal corps. As second in command of this platoon he fearlessly led them forward through heavy enemy fire, continually encouraging the men. Later he encountered deadly machine gun fire which reduced the strength of his command to but four men, and these were obliged to take shelter. The enemy machine gun emplacements, twenty-five yards distant, kept up a continual fire from four machine guns. After the fire had shifted momentarily. Corporal Turner rushed forward with fixed bayonet, and charged the position alone, capturing the strongpoint, with a complement of fifty Germans and four machine guns. His remarkable display of courage and fearlessness was instrumental in destroying the strong point, the fire from which had blocked the advance of his company.

His company having suffered severe casualties during an advance under machine gun fire, and finally stopped. Sergeant Sampler, then a corporal, detected the position of the enemy machine guns on an elevation. Armed with

German hand grenades which he had picked up, he left the line and rushed forward in the face of heavy fire, until he neared the hostile nest, where he grenaded the position. His third grenade landed among the enemy killing two, silencing the machine guns, and causing the surrender of twenty-eight Germans, whom he sent to the rear as prisoners. As a result of his act the company was immediately enabled to resume the advance.

Throughout the day the greatest confusion had existed at the command posts of the regiments and the brigade due to the lack of information regarding the progress of the attack. At first the information was highly favorable, both regiments reporting that they had reached their intermediate objectives. It already has been explained how this was in error. The maps provided were of such character that it was extremely difficult for the officers to ascertain exactly where they were and in their messages to their superiors they gave wrong locations.

Following the determined resistance met by the 141st Infantry and the complete halt of its attack, alarming reports were sent to the brigade commander by officers of the Second Division. These messages explained that the casualties had been extremely heavy, that ammunition was low and that the assaulting units were engaged on three sides. It soon became evident that all three lines of the attacking troops had become merged into one. This left the back areas without any steadying forces in the event it became necessary to retire before an enemy counter attack and to overcome this situation the commanding general of the Second Division placed two battalions of the Second Engineers at the disposal of General Whitworth, one to be placed in each regimental sector.

Learning of the conditions in the area of the 141st Infantry General Whitworth directed Colonel Jackson to go to the front line in person and see to its reorganization. At the same time various steps were taken to ascertain the correct positions occupied by the troops as the messages were so conflicting in regard to these. According to the information sent from the rear the right of the 141st Infantry at the close of the day was almost a mile in front of the 142d Infantry right, and the left of the 141st Infantry was several hundred yards in front of the 142d Infantry center. In reality the left of the 142d Infantry was north of the village of St. Etienne while the center and right dropped back rapidly from the cemetery to the east of the town to positions about 500 yards in front of the point where the right of the regiment had jumped off during the morning. From this point the line of the 141st Infantry continued east and southeast along the St. Etienne-Orfeuil road, or in rear rather than in front of the 142d Infantry line.

Due to this mass of misinformation repeated calls for the artillery to register on the machine gun positions of the enemy in front of the 141st Infantry, remained unanswered. At the close of the day when this situation had been gone over, the brigade commander directed that personal reconnaissance of the front line of both regiments be made by Lieutenant Colonel Phillipson of the 142d Infantry. The intelligence section was called upon to get information from every part of the line and ascertain conditions as to the location of the enemy. The confusion, the night and the great loss among the officers made the accomplishment of these tasks almost impossible. The information gained was so slight that even next morning there was hesitation about using the artillery on the ground in front of the 141st, from which the most damaging machine gun fire was being directed against the troops who had advanced on the left.

Throughout the day there had been no time to consider fatigue. The excitement, the constant effort to advance under cover, the rapidly changing conditions and the realization that vigilance was the price of life, kept the men on edge until there was no thought of food. In the heat of the day, when they had become hot from physical action, the want of water was felt but the supply had been ample to last through most of this. With the coming of night and the blessed opportunity to rest there also came reaction and the gnawing hunger of men who had not tasted food since the early morning. Cans of corn beef, "corn willie," were opened, here and there some of the men had supplies of hard bread, "hard tack" which they shared with their fellows. Wounded men came in for their full portion and most of these had been sent to the rear earlier in the day. Those who had no meat secured the packs from the dead who lay about on the ground. But the want of water was most imperative. The salt in the meat made the pangs of thirst almost unendurable. The line was too thinly held to send details to the rear for water, however. The nearest supply was known to be more than a mile to the rear. Messages sent to the rear by the wounded to have water brought up by details failed to bring results. Finally a carrying party from the line was organized to go to the rear under the direction of an officer. Slowly the hours dragged by and then just before the dawn the party returned, staggering under the weight of cases of tomatoes. No water was to be had at the rear but the water in the cans served as well and nothing was ever more refreshing to the thirst of parched troops. They grasped the cans eagerly and drained them of their contents.

Through the hours of the night sleep had been secured by all not on duty. This had been little enough on account of the chill air and no blankets. Every other man in the line was required to remain awake and on the alert in anticipation of a possible raid by the enemy. Patrols were sent out constantly to make sure that the ground to the immediate front was clear of Germans. In the counter attack of the late afternoon it was known that some of the men had been cut off and the patrols in the early part of the night were directed to locate any of these if possible but there were no results from this. In the early hours of the morning the wounded were evacuated from the village of St. Etienne.

There was a shifting of forces all along the line during the night in order that some parts of companies might be reformed. Company D of the 142d

Infantry was organized in the area from which it had started during the morning and to which it returned after getting cut of its sector into that of the French. Gaps in the line were filled here and there and in doing this an amusing and interesting incident occurred. On the right of the sector occupied by the 142d Infantry it was necessary to rearrange the position to cover a decided gap. No one seemed to be in command so a private who had been in the kitchen as a permanent kitchen police during most of the training season, took charge in the darkness and told the men where to go. The authority indicated in his tones caused the rest of his fellows to address him as "Lieutenant," and, when an officer came along inquiring who was in charge of that particular point he was referred to the "lieutenant." Questioning the "lieutenant" he was entirely satisfied and it was not until morning that the men discovered that they had been under the command of a student cook. Later the man was decorated for his work.

Thus the night passed without unusual incident. The intermittent shriek of the shells overhead, the irregular bursts of fire from the machine guns, the constant appearance of German flares on the hill to the north of St. Etienne, and the stealthy figures of men moving here and there to accomplish their missions of reorganization were all. Nothing but the chill night air prevented sound slumber for those who could find the opportunity and some of these doubled themselves up in their tiny fox-holes to sleep in spite of the cold and the lumpy chalk upon which they lay.

Chapter Six - St. Etienne — (Continued)

The crashing of artillery shells along the entire front of the Seventy-first Brigade heralded the dawn on the morning of October 9. These for the most part were from the enemy's batteries, the fire of the Allied guns being withheld because of the lack of proper information as to the exact location of the front line. But this intense shelling did not catch the troops in the front line unawares. Before the dawn they had been aroused by their officers and were "standing to" in readiness for any development. In their training they had been taught that when the enemy laid down his barrage they were to go into their dugouts and wait for the barrage to lift and roll on. But there were no dugouts here. Each man could only burrow deeper into the little hole he had cut for himself and pray that the next one would not get him. This intense shelling lasted for at least thirty minutes and several casualties resulted. The small number of men wounded in proportion to the fire from the enemy's guns was remarkable however.

During the previous day it had been learned that to move in the open in any direction was to attract the fire of a half-dozen machine guns and perhaps light artillery. Under cover of night, however, the men and officers found that they could work with impunity just as long as they did not make too much noise and showed no lights. Feverish picks and shovels in hands that could not keep warm enough to maintain a tight grip on the handles of the implements, yet which somehow managed through sheer determination to keep at the task, cut out an irregular line of defense about the village of St. Etienne and then southeast in front of Hill 140, from whence it turned still farther southeast along the St. Etienne-Orfeuil road.

While these troops in the front line had been strengthening their positions as best they could, the officers from regimental command posts, under direction of the brigade commander, were locating their troops in the front positions and organizing those in the rear positions.

In the 141st Infantry sector the front line had been reconnoitered by Colonel Jackson in person, who then returned to his headquarters and directed that Lieutenant Colonel L. R. James proceed to the front line to take command of the troops there, two of the majors having been killed and the other sent to the rear, incapacitated. The visit of Colonel Jackson to the front line had failed to clear up the location of the units in so far as the use of artillery on the positions to the right of St. Etienne was concerned. The reports sent back to the brigade commander showed the 141st Infantry about one kilometer farther north, where another road ran east and west from St. Etienne, than it really was, along the St. Etienne-Orfeuil road. In the support positions the troops of the Second Division had been so placed that they would render assistance in the event of an attack by the enemy, the detachment of engineers taking position on the extreme right of the sector to maintain combat liaison with the French.

These positions were maintained by the troops throughout the greater part of the day. In the late afternoon it was planned to conduct an attack on a small scale against some enemy positions on the right that were delivering damaging fire into the French as well as the 141st Infantry lines. The small detachment picked to conduct the assault was placed in position and held in readiness for the time to attack. This hour was delayed twice by the French, who also had a detachment prepared to go forward in the assault and then the entire plan was abandoned because of the intense bombardment delivered by the enemy's artillery just a few minutes prior to the time for the attack to begin. Those officers who had led their troops forward in the gains of the day before, remained in command of the positions reached, in the right, left and center respectively.

In the 142d Infantry area, a third provisional battalion had been organized and placed in the trees on the north slope of Blanc Mont where the support battalion had been at the beginning of the attack the previous day. During the night the lines had been reconnoitered both by Major Morrissey and Lieutenant Colonel Phillipson and a detachment of Marine machine gunners as well as engineers from the Second Division had been sent into the village of St. Etienne to strengthen the positions there. The engineers were placed in the cemetery and the Marines in the line in front of the town.

After consulting Major Morrissey at the latter's headquarters. Lieutenant Colonel Phillipson returned to the command post of the regiment with the information that instead of being on a line parallel with the village of St. Etienne the troops of the 141st Infantry really were south of the extreme right of the 142d Infantry, In the meantime, however, an order had been sent from the brigade command post that an attack would be made the morning of October 9, to straighten the line so that the right and center of the 142d Infantry would be brought up even with the 141st line. Immediately upon reaching the regimental command post and communicating his information to Colonel Bloor, Lieutenant Colonel Phillipson reported to brigade commander but before he could return to the regimental sector the third battalion had been formed and started forward in attack.

In spite of the battering they had received the day before, the assault, conducted under the direction of Major Morrissey, was executed in splendid fashion. The battalion swept forward in waves of small columns and then in waves of skirmishers as first they encountered the enemy's artillery fire and then machine gun fire. Onward to the front line positions they came and passing through this line continued on out over the little plain to the east of St. Etienne. By the time they reached the front line already established they had suffered heavily from artillery and machine gun fire and as soon as they passed beyond this line they met such a withering fire from flank positions on the right as well as frontal fire that they were compelled to stop and take what shelter was to be found.

This attack was launched about 10:30 A. M. and lasted the better part of half an hour. During the entire morning the German batteries rained their missiles upon the open ground to the east of St. Etienne and in the afternoon they concentrated their fire on the village as well. During the next twenty-four hours, night and day there was no cessation in the shelling upon the village and during the greater part of the afternoon the firing was no less intense on the open ground to the east of the town. Remnants of the assaulting force which reached the line to be established, remained in position until darkness. With the carrying of wounded to the rear the line began to lose many of its effectives as well. In the middle of the night a force was sent from the First Battalion to strengthen the line but so badly chosen was the position and of such little tactical value that these men were returned to their positions of the night before.

The second night was much like the first. Spades and pick-mattacks were plied vigorously as soon as the evening had settled into darkness. In the late afternoon the entire command "stood to" in expectation of a possible attack by the enemy. Another barrage from the enemy's guns marked the close as well as the opening of the day and under the first cover of darkness the men again set to with a will to better their places of shelter from the enemy's fire. Not all of them had picks and shovels and to relieve this shortage many used their mess pans to scoop out the chalky earth.

The prospects of an attack from the enemy still loomed as a possibility. This was considered especially probable in view of the situation all along the front although these details were not made known to the men in the line at the time. At the time the Seventy-first Brigade drove forward in its attack to the east of St. Etienne, the First Division was hurling itself against the defenses of Hill 240 and similar fortified positions in the Argonne, against which the Thirty-fifth Division had been shattered and which were holding up the general attack between the Meuse and the Aisne Rivers. At this time the Seventy-seventh Division was meeting desperate resistance in the Argonne woods proper, and had a battalion cut off from the division in such manner that it was considered doubtful if any of its personnel would get out alive.

In the event the Texans and Oklahomans should break through at St. Etienne and push on over the Aisne it would mean that the entire scheme of defense in the Meuse-Argonne operation would have to be abandoned and perhaps carefully prepared defenses of the Kremhilde Stellung would avail nothing. To give way at St. Etienne would mean that the artillerymen of the Fourth French Army would be enabled to plant their guns and open a direct flanking fire against the German defenses in and around Vouziers and it was likely that the attempts to cross the Aisne at this point in a flanking movement would be entirely successful. To prevent this necessity demanded that the Americans must be held at St. Etienne a little longer or possibly pushed backward over the crest of Blanc Mont into the old Hindenburg Line. To accomplish the latter a gigantic counter-blow would be necessary while to make possible the former an attack on at least a small scale would be necessary since the allied possession of the town was a danger ever menacing the safety of the Hun lines in that vicinity. Every nerve quivering with the tense expectancy of any possibility, listening posts crawled back and forth in front of the Brigade sector through the entire night. It was determined that no sound of possible massing of German forces opposite would escape them and it was with genuine relief that the reports of all patrol leaders in the early hours of the morning were heard to give no indication of activity on the part of the enemy. Another indication considered as pointing out that the Germans would not attack was the appearance of three fires in the back areas of the enemy's lines. It was assured that one of these was the village of Machault and that the others might be either villages or stores farther to the northeast. Later it developed that all three fires were villages wantonly destroyed by the Huns who were getting ready to retire.

Hunger and thirst were more pronounced the second night, if possible, than during the first. Through the day the sun had been almost hot and some of the men had been able to secure additional sleep but the almost constant and uninterrupted presence of enemy airplanes overhead had rendered sleep scarce enough. But if they might sleep they could get no food. This had to be brought up in the night. Under cover of darkness details again went to the rear and carried cases of tomatoes and canned beef on their shoulders more than two miles to the places where their comrades stood watch. Never had tomatoes and canned meat tasted so sweet. And they probably never will taste so sweet again, to the men of the plains who held their rifles in readiness with one hand while they ate with the other. There was not enough for all so each man stinted himself that the others might have some. This second night the detail had been able to get a limited supply of water which had been hauled during the day to the position occupied by the supporting troops in the first day's formation.

During the night it had become generally known that the Second Division troops would leave the sector not later than the night of the tenth and that some of these would leave the night of the ninth. However to relieve the situation some of the other troops of the Seventy-second Brigade, Thirty-sixth Division, had arrived in the vicinity of Somme-Py and were ordered to support the positions occupied by the Seventy-first Brigade. Although this was known at headquarters it had not been communicated to the troops in the front line positions. These were too busy with the things in front of them to consider what might be taking place behind. The additional lights of burning villages in the direction of Grand-Pre and Vouziers lit up the heavens, and mingling with the flares which the Germans were sending up constantly to the immediate front, gave a lurid light that served to keep the attention of wakeful soldiers to the front.

When Thursday, October 10, dawned on the chilled troops it brought with it the necessity for additional shifting of positions. Rumors spread that there was to be another general assault by the brigade. In the 141st Infantry area a platoon from Company A, which had been in the support position since the initial attack the morning of the 8th, was placed in the gap at the right of the sector occupied by the Second Engineers. A portion of the regimental machine gun company also was placed here and machine gunners from the 132d Machine Gun Battalion were sent to other parts of the line to give it strength. In the 142d Infantry sector it was necessary to shift a part of the First Battalion, which contained as many men from the other battalions of the regiment as it did its own, to the cemetery to relieve the detachment of Second Engineers and Marine machine gunners there, and to place additional men in the line to the north of the village. These last were from the Third Battalion.

The rumors that the brigade was to attack were well founded. When the commanding general of the Second Division made known the fact that his forces were to be withdrawn from the sector he informed General Whitworth that the Seventy-first Brigade was expected by the French Corps commander to clear away the force of Germans north of St, Etienne as that position was holding up the advance of the entire corps. When the word was passed to the officers and men in the front line, there were those who shook their heads gravely and wondered as they looked askance at that gaping right flank that had never been covered, but there was no complaint. Every man knew that if the word came to "go over", even with no more definite instructions than had been given the first time, the brigade would go.

In the early hours of Thursday morning the detachment of the First Battalion of the 142d Infantry, moving to the left through the outskirts of the village of St. Etienne, made their way into the cemetery. To accomplish this it was necessary to move by ones and twos from one low place m the ground to another, now in a shell hole, now through a shallow trench and now flat on their faces in the slightest fold in the ground until all of them had reached the cover from view behind the buildings in the village. But this was only half the task of getting into the cemetery. To enter the strong point occupied by the engineers it was necessary to take the men from the village across a stretch of flat, open ground about fifty yards wide and exposed every moment to the fire of snipers and machine gunners as well as others armed with long range automatic Lugers.

Hardly had the detachment reached the shelter of a half-demolished shed in the village before apparently every piece of artillery in the German line opened on the village. The cemetery was still a quarter of a mile away. One thing was left to do. Into three entrances of an enormous dugout, located in the eastern end of the village, the troops plunged regardless of possible mine traps or gas which might have settled in the lower levels. As the last man disappeared inside the burst of a mighty shell riddled the framework of one of the doors. Probably in no part of the German line from the Alps to the Channel were there larger dugouts than those in the village. They were nothing less than caverns. The one into which the relief detachment hurried for shelter had three long passageways opening out from a large central chamber in which there were bunks for 200 men and office space enough for the headquarters of a division. Undoubtedly it had served this purpose while the town was in the hands of the Hun, Signs posted on the walls of the houses in the town and other indications told of a long established division headquarters. In the cemetery the grave of a division commander bore further evidence of this.

In all there were four of these great caverns in the village as well as several smaller ones. One of the best of these was selected by the battalion commander as his headquarters. This one was constructed with a concrete entrance and lined with corrugated iron. In some of the great caves women's garments were found indicating that the higher Hun commanders had not been without company during the long evenings when the Allied guns did not entertain them. A piano was found in one of the dugouts as well as other furniture taken from the better dwellings in the village. All of the caverns were lighted by electricity and in the winter these were much more comfortable places of abode than the houses in the village. In a house near the dugout where the commanders of the First and Third Battalions established their headquarters and where Colonel Bloor later placed the headquarters of his regiment, the French Medical corps had set up a first aid station, and here also had been gathered the bodies of perhaps forty Germans, who had fallen in the defense of the village.

For a time after the artillery had opened on the town the streets were filled with flying debris of the shattered buildings as well as the flying fragments of bursting shell and the fumes of the high explosive caused the men to clap their masks on and adjust them as soon as possible. The shed in which the detachment had been assembled as soon as the village was reached was subjected to a direct hit from an enormous shell and at the close of the bombardment was only a pile of broken timbers and crumbled brick and stone. Gradually the firing died down until only an occasional shell was being directed toward the town perhaps as often as one every two minutes. This was the time to move. In small groups of five or six men the detachment filtered out of the entrances to the cavern and around the corners of the buildings down the street to the edge of the village. Every little while the far away scream of an approaching shell sent the men flat on the ground or caused them to hug the walls of the buildings while the monster hurtled nearer and nearer. Perhaps it would fall 100 yards away toward the other side of the village and then every face would wear a derisive grin. Perhaps it would rend asunder the walls of a building across the street and then there would be a quick short laugh of relief with accompanying remarks that "the Dutch could come darned close without hitting."

Lt. Ben Kiehn, 142d Infantry. After coming out of the lines safely in October, 1918.

Each little group of the detachment would be halted at the edge of the village and then one man at a time, at irregular intervals they would dash across the open ground and into the shelter of the cemetery fifty yards away. Time after time as this was accomplished there would be a series of spurts where the bullets of machine gunners and snipers kicked up the dust in the road, just too late to get the dodging doughboy. After a time the men watching the effort began to look upon it as a sort of sport and some went so far as to make small wagers that the next man would get over the same as the others did. All of these bets were won by those wagering on the side of safety. Every man reached the cemetery with a whole skin. As the detachment reached the cemetery defenses one man at a time, it took up the positions that were being vacated steadily by the engineers, who were filtering out of the position by another route. Observation of the men making their way into the cemetery soon brought intense shelling from the enemy batteries. The entire wrath of the Hun artillerymen again was vented on that part of the village adjacent to the cemetery and the French side of the burial place was wrecked by the high explosive shells. Just as the detachment of engineers was getting away from the village the enemy's fire reached its greatest intensity. The town adjacent to the cemetery was converted into a chaos of splinters, dust and gas but the Hun was too late, the exchange of places had been completed.

It was still necessary to report the completion of the relief to battalion headquarters but instead of sending a runner with the message the commander of the detachment elected to go himself, as the situation required discussion with the battalion commander as to the distribution of troops along the line. Awaiting a lull in the firing the officer started for the village. As if the artillery pieces themselves had eyes they opened their horrors on the village before he could reach the edge of the cemetery. Again there was a lull and this time a dash for the village succeeded, the bullets of the machine gunners spattering in the dust of the road in vain. A shell screamed overhead and landed in the farther end of the village. Another block was covered and another shell crashed through the wall of the house where the officer had paused as the first shell exploded. A spurt of yellow liquid came from this one plastering the walls and street with mustard. Another block was covered and as if tracing the officer's footsteps a third shell broke in the street where he had dodged into a doorway to escape the burst of the second. This was the usual experience of every man who passed through the village during the three days that followed the capture of the town.

Completing his report and receiving additional instruction as to his mission in the cemetery the officer emerged from the battalion commander's dugout into the street where apparent quiet had succeeded the shelling of a short time before. It was the calm before the storm. Halfway down the street not one but a half-dozen shells sent their warning to the occupants of the village. And these were followed by others. The deafening roar of one who had not subsided before another stopped the ability of ears to distinguish sound. A dozen times within the space of two blocks the officer was flattened against a wall, crouching behind a corner or huddled in a hole while the shells spent their force against the masonry of the village. Finally dashing into the cemetery from the bullet swept open space, with his face somewhat begrimed and with a tiny splash of mustard between his shoulders the officer greeted his second in command and settled down to comfort in the German side of the cemetery. This incident is related only to show what the troops in the village were going through hour after hour as it was necessary for men to go here and there with messages and officers were required to make tours of inspection.

The German cemetery proved to be the safest place in the line. Here there were more than 2,000 German dead and although the shells from the enemy batteries ploughed craters on every side the cemetery itself was not touched. Troops in the other front line positions were not so fortunate although the shelling on all parts of the line was not so concentrated as on the village. Here the gas shell fell in such quantities that the fumes made it extremely uncomfortable in all positions as the wind shifting from time to time rolled the gas away from the town to the places where men were lying in foxholes along the line.

While the position of the cemetery was being taken over from the engineers, who also had men from the Seventy-first Brigade with them, the detachment from the Third Battalion was being filtered through the village, and then across the creek bed to the positions north of the town. Here the positions were more directly facing the line of trenches occupied by the Germans. At a disadvantage because their position was under observation by the enemy from several directions the men in this part of the line could only crouch in their holes and lay in readiness for the next move. To lift a finger above the ground was to invite close range sniping as well as machine gun fire.

Partly because it had been directed from the corps commander that the enemy positions to the north of the town would be reduced by the brigade and partly because the position occupied was all but untenable, an officer was sent out with six men in daylight to patrol and reconnoiter the ground along the road leading from St. Etienne to the north and ascertain as much as possible about the positions occupied by the Germans. Repeated reports that the enemy was retiring from this front had caused the order from the rear that contact was to be maintained at all times with the Germans and the instructions to the patrol leader was that he was to reach a position where he could get observation on the German trenches if possible. Crawling over every foot of the way the patrol made its way along a shallow ditch at the side of the road for a considerable distance in "no-man's-land." Suddenly from both sides and in front the little group became the target of the enemy snipers. Bullets in a perfect hail left the officer and four of his men on the ground while the other two made their way back as best they could. There was all the contact desired.

To make doubly sure that the village was under fire from the enemy lines the commanding general of the Second Division had sent an artillery officer into the town. This officer had ridden his horse to the edge of the village without getting hit although fired upon frequently. The horse was hitched to a post in the edge of the town while the artillery officer hurried to the dugout of the battalion commander. Satisfied as to the conditions he had observed he started to return on his horse only to find that while he was in the dugout at battalion headquarters his mount had been blown to atoms by a German shell. The bridle was still attached to the post. For the purpose of learning accurately the conditions at this point the chief of staff of the Second Division also visited the village at the time the relief in the cemetery was being conducted. After a brief conversation with the officer in charge of the relief detachment, he returned to division headquarters. Later he was decorated with the Distinguished Service Cross for this voluntary exploit.

Expecting that the attack on the enemy positions north of St. Etienne would develop at any time the troops along the whole extent of the brigade front were on a keen edge of expectancy during the entire morning and afternoon of October 10. In so far as possible the ground over which the advance would be made was reconnoitered and avenues of approach against the positions were picked out. The thing that puzzled both officers and men most was the fact that little or no firing was being conducted by their own artillery. Infrequently the guns at the rear were sending over shell to the back areas of the German lines but none against the positions in the immediate front from which so much trouble was coming. When in the afternoon of October 10 the artillery at the rear actually did open on the nearest enemy positions it strengthened the belief that an attack was to be launched at dusk. This assault however did not result. The artillery fire had been secured through the personal efforts of Colonel Bloor of the 142d Infantry, who had taken all responsibility for damage that might occur to friendly troops. Through the two days and nights following the attack it had not been determined that the line on the right of the brigade sector was not a kilometer in advance of the position actually held.

The third night after the beginning of the attack again was one of hunger and thirst. The supply of water in the village was confined to one well which had been tested by the French medical troops and this was difficult of access because of the constant shelling by the enemy batteries and the danger of losing men by sending them after water. During the lulls in the firing a small supply of water was brought from the well however and just before daylight a limited amount of corned beef was issued. This was the fifth day and night that the men had been without cooked food. In every captured position they had found cans of German solidified alcohol with which they had boiled coffee, the only warm food possible to procure. The nights were more miserable than the days. In addition to the necessity for constant watchfulness and patrolling it was impossible for one to sleep comfortably in the chill night air without covering other than the clothing worn during the day. Toward the morning invariably there was a chill mist which caused the men to shake and thresh their arms about in an effort to stimulate circulation.

During the night of the ninth all units of the Second Division were relieved from the entire brigade front. The engineers had been withdrawn by noon during the day and early in the evening the machine gunners had taken their guns and moved out to the rear. This left the infantrymen in the line holding the positions with their automatic rifles to replace the machine guns. In several places the light Maxim machine guns captured from the enemy were set up to be used as defensive weapons in the event of a counter attack and with the adjustment carried out the morning of the ninth the line presented a stronger organization than before. With a greater knowledge of the line than they had had when they first went forward in attack the men also had gained greater confidence. Thus while there was a general feeling of relief that the expected assault against the enemy positions to the north of St. Etienne did not develop yet it is assured that the men would have done as well or better than they did the first day.

Arrival of the Whole Division

Simultaneously with the movement of the Seventy-first Brigade from the area around Somme-Suippe to the front line positions, the balance of the Thirty-sixth Division still in the area around Pocancy, was started on its way to the vicinity of Vadenay, a hamlet about fifteen miles north of Chalons-sur-Marne. This was to be the location of the new division command post according to the orders received from the Twenty-first French Army Corps commander. Accordingly all the division sick were evacuated to the hospital, surplus property was stored in the Pocancy area and the march begun over the unimproved roads which traveled in a semi-circle northwest of Chalons-sur-Marne. By this time the Seventy-second Brigade was much better equipped for a march than had been the Seventy-first Brigade. There were more rolling kitchens and the regimental supply organizations were better prepared to move rations and munitions. However these troops were still handicapped in this respect to a certain extent. The 143d Infantry left part of its rations in the area near Pocancy while the 144th Infantry left part of its ammunition there. Teams were doubled in order to drag the wagons over the roads and details of infantrymen were necessary at frequent intervals to get the wagons out of mudholes into which they had sunk.

At this time the Seventy-second Brigade also was considerably larger numerically than the Seventy-first Brigade. It had a total strength of something more than 6,000 officers and men. Most of these officers had been with the brigade a long time and were familiar with their men as well as the officers of the neighboring units. In addition to the Seventy-second Brigade the supply train, the sanitary train, the ammunition train, the 131st Machine Gun Battalion and the balance of the field signal battalion made the march. Due to the mud which rapidly exhausted the strength of the men and animals the march was slow and accomplished with the greatest difficulty. The night of October 6, the headquarters detachment of the Seventy-second Brigade halted in the town of La Veuve, the 143d Infantry in La Veuve and Dampierre-au-Temple, the 144th Infantry at Ferme de Vadenay and the 133d Machine Gun Battalion at Cupearly. Only a few buildings were available in any of these places so the officers as well as the men were required to bivouac in the open.

During the day the advance echelon of division headquarters was established at Vadenay, the rear echelon at Pocancy not getting under way until the seventh. Before the men at headquarters could get settled at Vadenay additional instructions called for another movement of the troops to the area just north of Suippes and orders were sent out at 3 o'clock the morning of October 7, for this move to be accomplished. Although the march of the seventh was not long it was equally as difficult as that of the day previous so that the troops were all but exhausted when they arrived at their destination. Some difficulty was experienced in billeting the troops when they arrived in the area north of Suippes but finally the entire command was settled in old French rest billets in the territory north of Suippes and between that place and the ruins of Souain. Some of the men were required to live in shelter tents but most of them secured shelter in the rather insanitary wooden shacks.

Only the wagon transportation accompanied the troops on the march. The trains were dispatched to Suippes over the better roads and arrived ahead of the marching columns. Thus the balance of the division, less the 111th Engineers who had left the command in the Bar-sur Aube area, and the Sixty-first Artillery Brigade, which was still in the training center, was assembled near the area from which the men of the Seventy-first Brigade had made their march into their first fight. The evening of the seventh Major General Smith had learned unofficially that the Seventy-first Brigade was to assault the morning of the eighth, even before the troops in the line were aware of the program ahead of them. The afternoon of October 8, officers who had been sent forward to make a reconnaissance, brought back information of the splendid courage displayed in the assault as well as the fearful casualties that had been suffered.

The morning of October 8 the sanitary train passed from the control of the commander of trains and was placed at the direction of the division surgeon. Later it went to the vicinity of Somme-Py where it was used to evacuate the wounded. Headquarters of the sanitary train remained in the vicinity of Somme-Suippe with other rear echelons of the trains. The supply train after reaching Suippes was sent back to the railhead at La Cheppe, a small station on the railroad between Chalons and Suippes. This train also brought forward the water carts and rolling kitchens which had been stored at Jalons when the division moved. During the day the division ordnance officer took over the ammunition dump from the Second Division Ordnance Officer in the vicinity of Somme-Py and that night the 111th Ammunition Train in bringing up a supply of cartridges for the Browning machine guns and automatic rifles as well as grenades and pyrotechnics, came under shell fire for the first time.

In spite of this new experience it unloaded its supplies and returned to the rear areas without mishap and accomplished its mission in the most approved fashion.

Late in the evening of October 8, General Smith with his chief of staff was summoned to the command post of the Twenty-first French Army Corps where instructions were given for the complete relief of the Second Division, In the course of this trip to the corps commander's headquarters General Smith passed through the zone of the enemy's artillery fire with his automobile, the command post of the corps being only a short distance from Somme-Py. In his discussion of the situation the French corps commander explained that it had not been his purpose originally to have the Seventy-first Brigade relieve the entire front line of the Second Division and that the disposition of Brigadier General Whitworth's troops was not in accordance with his views. General Naulin explained to General Smith what was desired in the way of formations for the division and prescribed that the artillery of the Second Division should remain with the Thirty-sixth in the line. Also it was provided that the troops in the sector should remain under the command of Major General Lejeune until 10 o'clock the morning of October 10, when the command would pass to General Smith. General Lejeune also was to remain with the commanding general of the Thirty-sixth for twenty-four hours after the exchange of command and upon leaving was to provide a staff officer thoroughly familiar with the situation to remain with General Smith for another twenty-four hours.

Following out these instructions the 144th Infantry was sent forward October 9, to a point in the vicinity of Blanc Mont while the 143d Infantry went to a point to the east of Blanc Mont. These troops were able to travel in much better fashion than had the troops of the other brigade. Their rolling kitchens enabled them to carry cooked rations in addition to the emergency rations although they suffered from lack of water as had their comrades a few days before. By the night of October 9 some of these troops had entered the sector of the Seventy-first Brigade and a battalion of the 143d Infantry was placed in the positions vacated by the engineers in rear of the 141st Infantry. It was not until the following day however that the troops had reached a position where they might be sent to the relief of the units in the front line and there was considerable confusion the night of the tenth when some of the companies from the 144th Infantry came under shell fire on the northern slopes of Blanc Mont as they were taking up a position in support of the 142d Infantry.

The division machine gun battalion of the Second Division was relieved after considerable difficulty by the 131st Machine Gun Battalion, Major Ellis Stephenson in command, due to the fact that the Second Division machine gun officer could not be located nor could the commander of the Second Division Machine Gun Battalion be found in time to make the relief as scheduled. However all troops of the Second Division had been withdrawn from the sector the night of October 10 and the entire sector was ready to be taken over by the commander of the Thirty-sixth Division during the previous morning.

Vaux-Champagne, headquarters for several units.

Chapter Seven - St. Etienne and After

During the night of October 10, after the arrival of the units of the Seventy-second Brigade and the completion of the relief of the Second Division, there was a noticeable falling off in the enemy's volume of artillery fire. Up until midnight the firing along the front line was intermittent but in the hours after midnight the shells came with a regularity that was unbroken. Through the early part of the night the Germans in the immediate front continued to send up about the usual number of flares but in the early morning even these ceased to be as numerous. All of the shells which fell in the vicinity were of the largest caliber. The town of St. Etienne continued to be the chief target.

Going into the sector of the 141st Infantry the relieving troops of the 143d Infantry were disposed with the Second and Third Battalions in the first line of supports, under the command of Majors Horace B. Siebe and Joe T. Goodman, respectively, while the Third Battalion under Major William E. Lake, was located in a second position to the rear. In the sector of the 144th Infantry the disposition was carried out on a similar plan. In this regiment the First Battalion under Major Lloyd S. Hill took position on the northern slopes of Blanc Mont in about the position occupied by the support line the morning of the first assault, while the Second Battalion, under Major Clark M. Mullican, as well as the Third Battalion under Captain Henry H. Craig, took station farther back toward the positions on the top of the ridge. Two companies of the 133d Machine Gun Battalion were placed with each of these regiments, which also had their regimental machine gun companies.

During the relief there had been a few casualties from shell fire and in the 141st area the forward battalions had been annoyed considerably by the enemy's machine gun and sniper fire. Other units of the division had relieved corresponding units of the Second Division with more or less difficulty, due to the long range shelling, by the enemy's guns, of the positions in the vicinity of Somme-Py. Here an officer and five men of the Sanitary train had been killed by the explosion of one shell while several others were wounded.

While the troops of the Seventy-second Brigade were getting settled into their positions the night of the tenth, patrols from the units of the Seventy-first Brigade were patrolling the ground to the front along the Arnes, in the locality of St. Etienne and among the pine groves where the line ran to the southeast of the village. One of these patrol.= sent out from the position in the cemetery, just before daylight, returned with the information that a cry had just been heard from well up the creek bed toward the location from which the Germans had directed their counter attack the afternoon of October 8. For a few minutes all ears were strained to locate the cry and then faintly through the mist it was borne to the men in the shell holes: "Help, Americans, help me!" Ruses of the Germans had been recounted to the men too often for them not to consider this another trick of the Hun, but it also was known that some of the men had been wounded and perhaps cut off at the close of the attack on the eighth. Two men quickly volunteered to go out and locate the wounded man, if indeed it were such, or to determine if it were a German ruse. Melting into the mist they were gone but comparatively a short time before they returned, walking slowly under the weight of a man who clung to their shoulders as they carried him between them. The man proved to be Private William C. Schaeffer of Company A, 142d Infantry, who had been wounded in the knee by a piece of shell, the afternoon of October 8, and who had crawled into a dugout to hide when the counter attack caused the line to swing back and connect up with the other troops in front of Hill 140. He had heard the German troops all about him but dared not move out of his hiding place for fear of capture. Twice he had administered first aid to his wound and had managed to live on the emergency rations carried in his pack. Thirst finally had driven him from the dugout the morning of the eleventh when the sounds of firing and voices had ceased. He had crawled a considerable distance toward the American lines before calling for help. As he left his hiding place he had heard German machine gunners talking only a short distance away.

The first rays of the morning light were filtering through the mist as the patrol brought Private Schaeffer into the cemetery and about the same time all firing by the enemy machine guns ceased along the line. It was the first time that the firing had wholly stopped since the troops of the Seventy-first Brigade arrived on the line and the strange stillness could not be understood for some time. In the mist it was thought that the enemy had stopped firing because he could not distinguish targets at which to fire but this was contrary to custom. Patrols were sent out cautiously but none of these encountered the Hun although they found where he had been but a short time before.

During the day previous the French on either side of the division's sector sent in constant reports that the enemy was falling back, leaving only small machine gun detachments to delay the Allied advance. On the east the French had been able to advance until they were approximately abreast of the Thirty-sixth Division front line while those on the west had had little success in forwarding their position. Late in the afternoon of the tenth, it was reported that the French on the left were holding a line which ran northwest of St. Etienne but this was the same condition that had prevailed the day previous, when the French had been able to move up following the attacks of the Seventy-first Brigade.

During the afternoon of the tenth the commander of the Twenty-first corps had visited the headquarters of General Smith to hold a conference and insist that the brigades be placed side by side in the line as soon as possible. Also plans were worked out for the Seventy-second Brigade to attack the afternoon of the tenth at 17 o'clock (5 P.M.). In order to accomplish this the division operations officer prepared a comprehensive order directing the attack and had it distributed with maps. Regimental commanders upon receiving this order called their conferences with their battalion commanders and the preparations for the forward movement were rushed to completion. In this rush, however, there was the same lack of particular instruction to a degree that characterized the assault by the Seventy-first Brigade the morning of the eighth. The maps were not pasted together and the officers did not have sufficient opportunity to give instructions to their men. However, there had been greater opportunity for reconnaissance and the general conditions were much better known than had been the case with the other troops.

At the given hour the assault battalions of both regiments moved forward. The 143d Infantry on the right was directed to pass over the lines of the 141st Infantry and drive the enemy from his position in front of that sector. The same general scheme prevailed for the 144th Infantry with regard to the lines of the 142d Infantry. The objective given both regiments was the front line of the French on the right which was declared to be progressing in pursuit of the slowly retreating enemy. This was in compliance with orders from the corps commander to the effect that the advance of the Thirty-sixth would be governed by the advance of the French units on either side.

In the gathering darkness the success of the attack did not develop. On the right the 143d Infantry had trouble in locating the front line. Through the gaps that existed there the assault battalion passed parts of the line without knowing it and then thinking it best to make sure of its position before advancing farther, halted for the night. These troops already had been under artillery fire while in support of the 141st Infantry the day and night previous and had suffered several casualties. In the advance the afternoon of the tenth they had encountered gas shells and had made part of the advance while wearing gas masks.

On the left the 144th Infantry started its attack simultaneously with a burst of shelling from the enemy's long range artillery. Some of these shells fell directly among the advancing elements and wrought general confusion. The result of this was that the leading battalion halted on the line from which the assault battalion of the 142d Infantry had jumped off the morning of the eighth. From this position patrols were sent out in the night, the troops being under the impression that they were in the front line, and the position was occupied throughout the night. In the early hours of the morning members of the intelligence section of the 144th Infantry, patrolling to the front encountered the detachment of the 142d Infantry in the cemetery to the east of the village and then returned with their information regarding the location of the actual front line. While one battalion was locating along the jump off line directly south of the village another had posted itself to the south of Hill 140 where it would have shelter from the enemy's machine gun fire.

Units of the 133d Machine Gun Battalion had been assigned equally to the two infantry regiments but encountered considerable difficulty in maintaining liaison in the night. One of the companies completely lost touch with the infantry to which it was assigned and did not regain communication until the morning of the eleventh.

There were several gas casualties reported to the dressing stations during the afternoon but most of these were of a slight nature and some of the men were returned for duty in the line where they had suffered only from the fumes of high explosive shells. The effect of the high explosive vanished with a short rest where the sufferer could have fresh air.

The night of the tenth the service of supply had considerable difficulty in bringing up stores to the units of the Seventy-second Brigade due to the confusion that existed when the passage of lines was not completed. The water supply was depleted among the men in the line and fresh water was not made available. Also there was a shortage of ammunition as well as food. Many of the men opened their reserve rations to satisfy the pangs of hunger. This confusion at the rear was largely responsible for the lack of food among the units of the Seventy-first Brigade, holding the front line.

During the operations of the Seventy-first Brigade as well as the fighting that followed later the Medical Corps troops of the division rendered the most excellent service. Accompanying the infantry in the face of machine gun and artillery fire, they took as many chances as the latter in the first day's fighting and thereafter came under the heaviest kind of shell fire time and time again. One of the first men killed the morning of October 8, was Captain Hanson, on duty with the assaulting battalion of the 142d Infantry. Numerous others among the Medical corps were wounded and time and again they were made the targets of the enemy in spite of the Red Cross bands they wore on their arms.

The work of the ambulances was remarkable. These drove direct to the regimental dressing station of the 142d Infantry to carry away the wounded of that regiment and the 132d Machine Gun Battalion. In the sector of the 141st Infantry this was not possible but aided by the litter bearers they hurried all wounded from that area as rapidly as they were brought back from the line, and given first aid treatment. At the triage established in a dugout near Somme-Py the wounded were given further attention before being sent to the hospitals. The most urgent cases were cared for first, and hurried away to the rear. Operations were performed where such were deemed necessary and ceaseless work on the part of the surgeons cared for the hundreds of wounded in a remarkably short space of time. At night there were no lights at the dressing stations and the task of dressing wounded was rendered doubly difficult. So good was the work of the Medical Corps that about two hours was declared to be the average time which elapsed from the wounding of a man in the line to his arrival at the triage near Somme-Py, a distance of three or four miles. As the result of this most of the patients arrived at the base hospital in excellent condition and the saving of life was at the maximum.

Throughout the fighting the detachment of the field signal battalion on duty with the Seventy-first Brigade, had been busily engaged in keeping up the wires between the various command posts. The morning of the tenth telephone wires were strung into the front line positions, one station being established in the foxholes on Hill 140 and another at the battalion headquarters in St. Etienne. Two others were established along the front of the 141st Infantry. The men who ran these lines of wire and made repairs where the wires were cut by the bursting shells, were constantly under fire and their work took them to the very front lines day and night. Sometimes the same line would have to be mended five or six times. Each time the linesmen would have to search along every foot of the wire until they came to the broken place which had to be joined with the loose end of the other part of the line. To accomplish this in the dark required the greatest patience as well as hardihood. The signal platoons of the infantry regiments assisted in this work and were constantly on duty with their respective organizations in the front lines.

The intelligence sections of both infantry regiments were greatly handicapped in the first two days fighting around St. Etienne and to the east along the front of the 141st Infantry. They gained little information from the Second Division and the confusion which followed the assault the morning of the eighth left them at a disadvantage not overcome until two days later. However through the work of the scouts and observers who patrolled the entire brigade front something was learned of the disposition of the enemy's troops, especially his machine gun nests and advanced artillery positions. Much of this work was done by the intelligence officers in person. Advancing with the assault waves many of the scouts were wounded and the organization badly crippled. One of the scout officers in the 142d Infantry was badly wounded when he took charge of a disorganized platoon and led it forward after its commander had been wounded and sent to the rear.

When the sun had cleared the mist away from the low ground along the Arnes the morning of October 11, the slopes of the ridge to the north of St. Etienne were found to be utterly devoid of the machine gun nests that had proved such a menace to the troops in the front line the day before. Since the early dawn there had been no firing and patrols had reported all signs of the enemy gone. On either side the French could be seen advancing boldly toward the north and about 10 o'clock the forward battalions of the Seventy-second Brigade passed through the advance positions of the Seventy-first Brigade and took up the advance toward the town of Machault, the direction of the division having been changed from slightly northwest to northeast. This change had been occasioned by the fact that it no longer was necessary to continue the effort to cut off the German forces in the vicinity of Reims, the enemy having withdrawn along that front.

With the forward positions taken over by the Seventy-second Brigade the commanders of the Seventy-first Brigade units immediately took up the task of reorganizing their commands. The men of the two regiments had become so mingled into detachments that it was necessary for each battalion commander to establish an assembly point and call for the officers and men of his battalion to gather there. After this had been accomplished each company commander had to separate his men from the others. In some, instances these companies were formed by sergeants, all of the officers having been wounded or killed. Where this proved the case officers were borrowed from other companies to take charge. Hardly any of the companies had more than one officer and none had more than two officers, after this readjustment.

This reorganization consumed the greater part of the afternoon and was supervised in person by the regimental commanders. Most of the battalions were commanded by captains, the one exception being the Second Battalion of the 142d Infantry, commanded by Major Morrissey. During this time the area was under fire only from the longest range guns and the shells fell at irregular intervals, being infrequent and directed for the most part at the town of St. Etienne. The shelling was from a new direction, the firing apparently being done by long range artillery located near the Aisne River in the vicinity of Vouziers.

The night of the eleventh the troops in the front line were fed the first warm food they had tasted since the morning of the sixth when they had been given their breakfast in camp near Somme-Suippe. During the entire time they had been in the fighting zone they had lived on canned meat and tomatoes for the most part with a small amount of French bread which they carried up from the rear with the greatest difficulty at night. In the meal served the night of the eleventh they were given steak and vegetables in quantities to appease the most ravenous and then all lay down to enjoy the first comfortable sleep they had been able to get for a week. With only a gas sentry posted for each company, the men dug comfortable holes in the ground and lined these with pine needles over which they piled overcoats and blankets that they had taken from the German dugouts or from the few packs that were available.

In the meantime the officers were busy counting the dead and accounting for the wounded and missing. They had not seen parts of their companies and platoons for more than two days, having been separated in the fighting early during the morning of the eighth. Officers had to go from one end of their regimental sectors to another in the effort to locate all of their troops and in some instances the soldiers of the two regiments became intermingled. Also some of the men became identified with machine gun platoons and remained with them. It was in this counting of noses that many wounded were accounted for the first time. As the troops were gathered together they told of the fighting in this and that part of the field and how this or that man had been killed or wounded and evacuated to the rear.

The casualties had been frightful. The full extent of these now became known for the first time. In the 141st Infantry there had been 109 officers and 2,469 men when it entered the lines the night of the sixth. Of these seventy-eight officers and 1,789 men remained at the close of the fighting on the tenth. Of the ninety-one officers and 2,333 men who were reported with the 142d Infantry the morning of the seventh, fifty-three officers and 1,690 men remained the morning of the eleventh. In the 132d Machine Gun Battalion there had been thirty officers and 712 men to enter the battle and at the close there remained twenty-one officers and 600 men. These figures include all forces such as the supply troops and the troops at the headquarters of the various organizations. It is estimated that only about 1,700 officers and men actually engaged in the fight for the 142d Infantry which lost approximately nine officers killed; thirty-two officers wounded; 147 men killed; and 635 men wounded or missing in action. Some of these missing were prisoners captured in the German counterattack the afternoon of the eighth, but the greater number had been wounded and some never were accounted for. It is assured that they were killed by some of the larger enemy shells.

Those actually participating in the fighting in the 141st Infantry numbered a little less than 2,000 men and officers and the losses in that regiment were only slightly less than in the 142d Infantry. The final reports on the casualties of the four days before St. Etienne showed the losses of the 142d Infantry to be something more than 800 officers and men and the losses of the other regiment to be something more than 700 officers and men. The losses in the machine gun battalion had been comparatively heavy considering the number of men engaged.

When the units were organized the afternoon of October 11, battalions appeared about the size of a full company while regiments were only slightly larger than full strength battalions. In the faces of the men gathered together in the depleted ranks could be read the strain of the past week but at the same time the faces wore the expression of tried soldiers that would not be found wanting in any task that might be assigned to them. They greeted each other solemnly and each man respected the others in a manner new to them.

The first task of the relieved troops the morning of October 12 was to gather together and bury the dead. Details of men from each organization were sent out under an officer to locate the fallen of their own command. These were brought together at once place for the most part and interred under the personal supervision of the officer who would be assisted by the regimental chaplain. The duties of the latter were to take charge of any valuables that might be found on the persons of the dead and to perform the religious rites prescribed by the regulations. In a few instances the fallen were laid to rest where they were found, the time allotted for the task not permitting them to be carried to the common burying place. Wooden crosses were erected over each grave and the identification of the man was fastened to his cross. Marines as well as the French were also taken care of by the burying parties of the Seventy-first Brigade.

The Advance of the Seventy-Second Brigade

In the meantime the advance of the Seventy-second Brigade had begun. Its commander had been instructed to pursue the retreating enemy and attack with all possible vigor wherever the Germans could be found. In both the infantry regiments the formation for this advance was practically the same as had been the case the afternoon before during the attempted passage of lines. The forces of the 143d Infantry required considerable reorganization before the advance could be taken up but as early as 9 o'clock one company of the 144th Infantry had entered the cemetery to the east of St. Etienne and passed on over the Arnes. This was one of the companies of the First Battalion which took over the positions occupied by the 142d Infantry in the village and then pushed on to a position to the north of the town.

A short time later the Second Battalion of the 144th Infantry emerged from its positions behind Hill 140 and advanced over the flat to the east of St. Etienne, passing through the right of the 142d infantry sector. Advancing over the Arnes it became the leading battalion of the regiment, the First Battalion taking the support position and the Third Battalion the reserve position. Until the Second Battalion reached a point almost two kilometers north of St. Etienne it did not come in contact with any of the enemy's troops. However, at the top of the ridge about half way between St. Etienne and Machault, its scouts drew fire from several machine gun nests located on either side of the narrow gauge railroad that was operated by the Germans to carry ammunition and other supplies from Machault to the positions in the old Hindenburg line. Immediately these positions were uncovered the task of reducing them was begun. Flankers soon brought fire to bear that enabled the troops in front to advance. During this skirmishing, which lasted more than an hour, enemy observation was secured by an airplane which appeared overhead, and almost immediately this was followed by artillery fire that brought numerous casualties within the ranks of the attacking force. During the artillery fire two small ammunition dumps, abandoned by the enemy, were exploded in the vicinity, causing the impression generally that the ground was mined. To add to the difficulties of the situation the assaulting troops came under fire from the right flank, in the sector of the 143d Infantry, which ground had not yet been reached by that organization. Company C of the First Battalion was sent into the gap to the right to aid Major Mullican's Second Battalion in the attack but arrived in position simultaneously with the advance elements of the 143d.

During the artillery fire some of the German machine gunners apparently withdrew to positions held by the enemy in Machault while others were shot or bayoneted at their posts, being unable to get away before their positions were reached. Some of the men in the 144th assault waves told of machine gunners who held their positions and actually fired their Maxims until they were killed, one actually being bayoneted by a flanker who had gained the rear and killed the operator of the machine gun in his seat.

When these positions had been overcome the assault battalion continued the advance until about a kilometer south of Machault, where it came under machine gun fire from positions in and around the town. Some of the machine guns were planted in the upper stories of the houses while others were located to the east and west of the town. This fire was returned by the assaulting troops as soon as they could get into such positions as would allow them to bring their rifles and automatic weapons to bear. But the advancing infantrymen were spared any real effort directed to dislodge the enemy. The German's own artillery suddenly opened on the town and caused the "boche" machine gunners to scurry away to the north in order to save their lives. Due to this kindly aid from the Hun artillery, Machault was evacuated before an assault could be launched against it. Almost immediately afterward the enemy ceased altogether to direct his artillery on the positions in the vicinity, apparently being uncertain of the location of his own lines and being afraid to fire at random. As soon as the enemy's fire had been silenced the advance elements of the 144th passed through the town and beyond several hundred meters to the north and northeast, where the regiment was halted for the night. In passing through the village great care was taken to see that no hidden positions of the enemy were remaining to open fire on the rear of the advancing troops after they had gone beyond.

While this advance was being conducted the 143d Infantry was moving forward in the adjoining sector to the east. Due to the widely scattered detachments of this regiment in the front line positions the night of the tenth, there had been little time to issue orders in written form. Instead the regimental commander had called his officers into a conference where he told them the plan of the advance. The same formation as that used the previous day was carried out and the forward movement begun as soon as possible. The assault battalion was under the command of Major Siebe who did not get his instructions until after the hour designated to start. This necessitated a slight delay in addition to that occasioned by the confusion of the night before.

In its advance the 144th Infantry had been able to move out abreast of the French after the first kilometer but the 143d was practically a kilometer in rear through the greater part of the morning. Shortly after noon however it came abreast of the French division on the right although not quite up with the advance elements of the 144th Infantry. No resistance was encountered by the 143d until it moved up even with the established front. A little more than two kilometers north of the old line east of St. Etienne, the French had encountered a line of enemy machine guns which held up the attack along the St. Etienne-Semide road. The advance units of the 143rd Infantry encountered these upon coming alongside the advance French elements. Company I of the 143d acting in conjunction with the French, soon overcame these however and the advance continued.

Upon approaching the line running east and west through the village of Machault the forward battalion came under fire from the German positions in the town but little damage was done as the enemy artillery began to bear on the village almost immediately. The right flank of the regiment had been subjected to fire from wooded positions to the east of Machault at the same time. These last positions were in the sector of the Seventy-third French division on the right, which had not yet reached the line running through the town. The fire from the wood ceased a short time after the enemy had been routed from the village and soon afterward the French advanced on a line with the 143d. which was still somewhat in rear of the 144th Infantry and the French on the left.

During the advance the companies of the 133d Machine Gun Battalion remained on duty with the units of the two regiments to which they had been assigned or the attempted passage of lines at St. Etienne, and when the troops halted for the night in the vicinity of Machault they took up positions slightly in rear of the front line where they would be effective against any counter movements on the part of the enemy.

Immediately after the arrival of the 143d Infantry the enemy could be observed moving to the rear from positions directly to the front of the 144th Infantry. The advance detachments of this regiment opened fire and some of the officers urged that a further advance be taken up in order to demoralize this withdrawal. This was not attempted however due to the lack of liaison with the troops on either side and to the rear. The lines to the rear had been extremely difficult to maintain during the advance and in the night the French moved forward approximately two kilometers without giving any intimation of what they were doing.

After dark an effort was made to bring up the rolling kitchens and prepare sufficient hot food for the personnel of both regiments, as well as the machine gun battalions, but this was not wholly successful. The troops in reserve, who were close to the kitchens were fed but the other battalions had to depend on their reserve rations. Water also was scarce although a small supply was distributed among some of the units. At times during the night it was reported that enemy snipers had obtained positions in the village of Machault and were firing on the Americans near the town but patrols failed to locate any of these and if they were there they made good their escape.

In the night the command posts of both regiments were moved forward in order that the regimental commanders could be in closer touch with the advancing troops. In the 143d Infantry the colonel, however, did not confer with his battalion and company commanders until daylight, having passed the night in visiting the front of the entire brigade. During the advance the regiment had been under the personal direction of Lieutenant Colonel Taylor, the regimental commander remaining at the established command post until it should be moved forward.

It is estimated that the total number of casualties resulting from the advance of the Seventy-second Brigade to the vicinity of Machault, was in the neighborhood of 200 for both regiments of infantry and the machine gun battalion. Most of these had resulted from the enemy's artillery fire, the resistance by machine gunners and snipers having been slight in the extreme.

Arriving at Machault the troops entered a more fertile country than had been around them at St. Etienne and Blanc Mont ridge. This was the upper Champagne where the underbrush vied with the pine growths in covering the ground, and where there was a rank growth of weeds in the open places although there was no cultivation. The last was not encountered until the final stretches of the broad plateau were crossed just before the sharp outline of the Aisne valley was reached. The town of Machault itself is on the main highway from Reims to Verdun and was used for the four years of the war as a distribution point for the entire German forces in the Champagne. A broad gauge railroad operating into the town from the north, transferred its freight to narrow gauge roads at this point while in the Mont St. Remy, a short distance to the northeast, the enemy had maintained an ammunition dump of gigantic proportions. From it in every direction toward the battle lines there had operated narrow gauge railroads. But even this gigantic dump had not contained all of the munitions the Germans planned to use. In the woods on both sides of the little branch lines were piled tier after tier of artillery shells as well as boxes of small arms ammunition. Apparently there had been an effort to remove some of this but the task was too colossal in the short time allowed by the determined assaults of the Allied arms. In addition to the ammunition there were piles and piles of other material such as lumber and stores used in construction work. The woods literally were full of German property for which the French later gave the Thirty-sixth Division commander a receipt for approximately $10,000,000 this being the minimum estimate of the property's worth. Testifying to the haste with which the "boche" had been compelled to leave these supply dumps, some of the tram cars still laden and on the way to the front lines were standing ready to continue the journey.

To the north of Machault the ground is flat for some distance before it breaks up into a series of knolls and little valleys south of where the broad valley of the Aisne is reached. In this flat country are the villages of Dricourt. Leffincourt and Pauvres, while to the north of them, hidden in the tiny draws that mark the abrupt meeting of the plateau with the valley of the Aisne are the towns of Vaux-Champagne and Coulommes. In the valley of the river and under clear observation from the opposite slopes to the north are the towns of Mont Laurent, Saulces Champenoise, Saint Vaubourg, Chardeny, Chuffilly, Mery and La Roche as well as other little hamlets, around which the Germans had caused the Russian prisoners of war to cultivate the crops. On the banks of the Aisne and its accompanying Ardennes Canal are the towns of Givry, Attigny and Rilly, the last named being in a loop of the river. Of these the more important is Attigny, which had a population of several thousand people before the war.

The Advance of the Entire Division

Into this territory the Seventy-second Brigade again took up its advance the morning of October 12. Back at St. Etienne as the details were about the business of salvaging the property strewn about the fields and burying the dead, the reorganized units of the Seventy-first Brigade were getting under way to follow up the advance of the other half of the division. Before the continuation of the movement forward the 142d Infantry received a splendid tribute from the commanding officer of the French division on the left. The latter declared that the work of the American regiment in holding the ground around St. Etienne in the face of the enemy's bombardment and counter-attack, after the unfavorable manner in which the assault had been launched was nothing less than marvelous. For the work of the whole Seventy-first Brigade at this point the entire division received a citation. It was here that the long hours of training for more than a year in the camps of Fort Sill and Fort Worth as well as in the Thirteenth training area told their true value. When officers had been killed and wounded until none was left, the troops had been taken in hand, by sergeants, corporals and sometimes privates who handled the situation in a manner creditable to the best troops in the world. No enlisted men ever showed to better advantage.

After a week of the greatest hardship, one hot meal had served to bring the spirit of the entire brigade back up to normal and as the columns moved out across the ground between St. Etienne and Machault there were songs keeping cadence with the marching feet and jokes were bandied about as though they had spent the day before in New York or Paris, There were not as many to sing but they sang with the same spirit as when they marched into battle the first time in their lives, just the week before.

In the advance northward from St. Etienne the columns again left the highways as they had done in the march from Suippes to Somme-Py but this time the marching was not so difficult. The ground was firmer and there were not so many entanglements to bar the path. Some time during the night of the eleventh all shelling has ceased in the vicinity of St. Etienne, even the longest range guns apparently having been moved back to a point where they could not be brought to bear on this part of the line.

At this time the troops in the First American Army, to the east across the Aisne, had pushed forward to the Kremhilde Stellung, the First, the Thirty-second, the Forty-second, the Seventy-seventh and other divisions having rolled back the stubborn Hun until he was ensconced behind this last barricade between the Allies and Sedan. Montfaucon, so long the headquarters of the Crown Prince, long since had been in the hands of the Thirty-seventh Division and the troops that succeeded that organization in the line. The Thirty-second, the Ninetieth and other divisions were being placed in positions of readiness to hurl themselves against the enemy in this last stronghold and drive him beyond his railroad centers at Sedan and Mezieres, and perhaps cut off the retreat of the German forces in Flanders. The last weight of the Allies was being applied to break the German line and end the war. But these things were unknown to the men of the Thirty-Sixth as they plodded ahead over the shell torn surface of the upper Champagne.

As the Seventy-first Brigade was moving out of its positions of the night before the assaulting echelons of the Seventy-second Brigade were taking up the further advance from their positions near Machault. During the night the French on either side had moved to the front and the forward troops of both regiments were urged to move up even with them. High overhead the "sausage" balloons of the enemy always were visible and as soon as the advance began long range artillery started to register among the deployed elements. Now and then the advance would be held up by isolated machine gun positions but these were overcome without great difficulty. As the town of Machault had been destroyed by flames so had other villages in the area, although Dricourt and the towns farther north had been spared. Every joint of the standard gauge railroad had been blown up, so that it was rendered wholly useless until it could be repaired. In this way the enemy kept it from being available to move the heavier pieces of artillery which had to be brought up from the rear. Much of the rolling stock for this road was found to be serviceable and later the road was repaired to an extent where it could be used by the French.

Throughout the morning the planes of the Allies as well as the enemy were busy in their maneuvers above the advancing lines. On both sides the chief effort was directed toward the destruction of the observation balloons. Late m the afternoon some of the Allied air pilots were successful in setting fire to one of the German "sausages" which soon plunged earthward in a mass of flames. Apparently the observers were caught in the wreckage as no one was seen to leap and descend by means of the parachute. The next morning practically the same thing happened to one of the allied balloons. These performances were watched with the keenest interest by the doughboys on the ground. When the Allied balloon was brought to the ground the lone observer managed to leap before the descent and landed on a spot not far from the location of the 142d Infantry. "That just about skins any circus trick I ever peeped at!" was the way one Texas cowpuncher summed up the performance. The men of the Thirty-sixth were seeing things every minute that outdid most of the Barnum wonders they had learned to marvel at in the piping time of peace. The Allied balloons kept pace with the advancing infantry without great difficulty. The marching of the latter was comparatively slow. Each balloon was anchored to a heavy motor truck which moved with remarkable speed along the better roads, especially in view of the wireless apparatus attached.

By the late afternoon the Seventy-second Brigade had advanced to a line running east and west through the town of Vaux-Champagne. in a little valley to the south of which the main body of the 144th Infantry took position during the night, after slipping to the east slightly to gel; into the proper sector of the regiment. The 143d Infantry was to the east of the town and somewhat more advanced than the 144th, it having placed outposts along the northern slopes of Hill 167, near Coulommes, from which the entire valley for many miles could be observed. This was the highest elevation in the vicinity and practically every foot of the enemy's territory across the Aisne could be observed on a clear day without difficulty. This part of the Aisne valley offered splendid protection and a varied assortment of positions which could be used to advantage from a defensive standpoint.

On the ground between the position of the 144th Infantry and the town of Vaux-Champagne the enemy had established an aviation field during the early years of the war but had abandoned it later for a field just south of Aitigny. In these aviation sheds some of the advancing troops found shelter for the night and escaped the rain that began to fall on their less lucky comrades during the afternoon. Most of the troops in the Seventy-second Brigade were suffering from want of water, the supply at Machault having been avoided for fear that it might have been poisoned by the fleeing "boche." No other opportunity had been afforded to get a supply. Also most of them had been without hot food and coffee. During the night this situation was relieved by the arrival of the rolling kitchens and water carts from the rear. Most of the men were given hot "chow" and made cheerful for the night in spite of the rain.

During the morning the Seventy-first Brigade had advanced until it reached the flat country just to the southeast of Dricourt where it took position among the pine groves out of sight of the enemy's planes and observers. There it remained through the balance of the day. The rolling kitchens were brought up to this point and after considerable difficulty a hot supper was served. Also a sufficient quantity of water was received. During the afternoon many of the men took occasion to shave and otherwise clean up. It was the first opportunity they had enjoyed in more than a week. Pocket mirrors were propped up in trees and water was heated with solidified alcohol, no fires being permitted. These troops by this time were entirely without shelter. In order to avoid the rain that was falling steadily they dug holes in the ground and covered these with pine boughs, which rendered the place water proof. Each man working for himself was rapidly assimilating the knowledge of how to look after his wants under the most trying circumstances.

Other units of the division, including the attached artillery brigade, began the movement forward with the Seventy-first Brigade. The going was especially difficult for the artillery. Unable to travel along the highways to the east, the heavy gun carriages and other vehicles frequently sank in the soft earth until infantry details were necessary to help the horses extricate them. These and the water carts as well as the rolling kitchens struggling forward through the mud made the infantrymen glad of their positions.

While the infantry of the Thirty-sixth had halted in the vicinity of Vaux-Champagne the afternoon of the twelfth the 141st French division on the right of the Seventy-third French division had reached the Aisne river, and French Cavalry from the left had patrolled to the town of Attigny which they found to be burning, the Germans having set fire to it in numerous places before leaving. In this town there were large powder magazines which the enemy had established as early as 1915 but these failed to explode. The bridges across the river and the canal had been destroyed everywhere, thus blocking the advance across the river. On the south bank much of the underbrush had been cut and piled on the north bank to give the enemy protection and at the same time leave the area of the Allies exposed to fire. Apple orchards in the vicinity of Attigny had been cut down as had the trees which lined the highways.

When the French cavalry patrol had entered Attigny it had been fired upon from the brickyard to the east of the town as well as from the sugar mill in the west end of the town. Later the sugar mill was abandoned by the enemy but the Germans remained in position in the elbow of the river just to the east of Attigny and in which were Rilly and Forest Ferme, the last of which was the scene of the final fighting of the Seventy-first Brigade,

The night of the twelfth the corps commander directed that the commanders of all divisions in his corps make effort to cross the river and establish bridgeheads with a view to pursuing the enemy on the north bank. Due to the fact that his forces were taking over the sector of the Seventy-third French division on the right, General Smith was not able to carry out these instructions as prescribed by the corps commander but the commanding general of the Seventh French division on the left announced his intention of making a surprise crossing the morning of the thirteenth in the vicinity of

Givry, and called upon the Thirty-sixth for the assistance of its heavy artillery. This was placed at the French division commander's disposal.

During the morning of Sunday, October 13, the troops again were in movement forward, this time with the intention of placing the brigades side by side in the line as had been planned originally by the corps commander as well as the division commander. The orders prescribed that the Seventy-first Brigade would be on the right of the sector and would occupy the territory between a point slightly west of Attigny to a point about halfway across the front of the enemy positions in the elbow of the river. West of Attigny and about a kilometer west of the town of Givry was to be the front of the sector occupied by the Seventy-second Brigade. In the Sector of the Seventy-first Brigade the 141st Infantry was on the right and the 142d Infantry on the left, while the Seventy-second Brigade was disposed with the 143d Infantry on the right and the 144th Infantry on the left.

During the early hours of the morning the troops began to move forward to their positions. The Seventy-second Brigade completed its movements about noon, but the other brigade which had farther to march was not in position until nightfall. Part of the movement was continued into the night during which the enemy began once more to shell the area, but with little apparent damage. Headquarters for the Seventy-first Brigade was established in the town of Vaux-Champagne as was the artillery brigade headquarters and the headquarters of the 142d Infantry. Division headquarters had been established in the town of Dricourt. Here the engineers also were established and began their work of repairing the roads in the vicinity as well as patrolling the river and canal with the view to constructing bridges across these in the event bridgeheads were obtained. The command post of the Seventy-second Brigade originally had been placed in Vaux-Champagne also but it later was moved to Pauvres.

The troops of the division were disposed in three zones along the entire front. The forward zone along the canal and river was known as the outpost zone and this ran back from the river for a distance of from two to three kilometers. Back of this was the zone of supports and back of this the reserve and main line of resistance in the event of an attack. The troops in the outpost zone were widely scattered, much of the territory near the river being covered by patrols. In this manner a close watch was kept of the enemy across the river and at the same time the danger of casual ties was lessened to a great degree.

During the advance from St. Etienne lo the river, the supply department had labored under the greatest difficulties. The poor roads and the congestion of traffic rendered the movement of supplies impossible in some cases but the addition of a considerable number of water carts and rolling kitchens relieved the situation to a great extent. There were not enough of these kitchens to provide one for each company but there were enough for the depleted number of troops to be fed so that at least two warm meals each day could be served. Water was plentiful in the region and the troops no longer suffered from this.

In this movement to the Aisne the hospital and ambulance units were brought up from Aulnay, where they had been left when the division first started into the front line. All of the sick at Aulnay had been evacuated to the base hospitals or returned to their regiments. The hospital then was established in the vicinity of Machault. The supply dump also was moved up to a position near Coulommes while the ammunition dump was placed in the vicinity of Dricourt. Frequently the ammunition train in bringing up munitions from the rear came under fire from the enemy's batteries. These also constantly made the service of supply hazardous. Most of the hauling was done at night, the men and animals resting during the day.

Chapter Eight - The General Advance

All units of the division having been located in their new sectors along the Aisne river there was a general shifting of command posts and adjustment of supply services to the rear. The commanders of the 142d and 143d Infantry regiments maintained their headquarters in the town of Vaux-Champagne. The 141st Infantry established its P. C. at Coulommes et Marquent and the 144th Infantry command post was located at Moscou Ferme. This necessitated some shifting of regimental aid stations as well as locations for kitchens and dumps from which supplies were distributed. Due to the fact that many troops constantly were making their way in and out of Vaux-Champagne, where the artillery brigade headquarters was located as well as the command post of the Seventy-first Infantry Brigade, the town was subjected to heavy shelling by the enemy but with comparatively few hits. Most of the shells fell on the ground in the vicinity.

The railhead of the division remained at La Cheppe, some forty miles away over roads that in many places were extremely difficult of passage, due to the heavy shelling they had undergone. In spite of this handicap the supply department so arranged its schedule that the troops in the front line positions were provided with the garrison ration of fresh meat and bread with but little irregularity. Also the supply of water carts was increased to the extent that those which had been borrowed in the area around Somme-Py were returned to their owners as were other similarly borrowed supplies. Within a short time the division also received an additional supply of automatic pistols and these were distributed without loss of time. All Browning automatic rifles were placed in the hands of troops, none being held in reserve, as had been the case when the command went into action the morning of October 8. All of these automatic arms that had been cast aside by wounded in the first fighting before St. Etienne also were gathered up and after being repaired or cleaned were placed in the hands of the troops who had learned by this time to give them their true value.

The period from October 13 to October 27, is described as a period of quiet for the units along the Aisne at this point, although it proved to be anything but quiet along the banks of the river and the canal where the patrols? of the enemy were constantly coming in contact with the patrols of the Thirty-sixth and the French. The first two days after the division took up its position this activity was not so pronounced, but later when the efforts to gain information of the enemy across the stream were more determined, frequently there were clashes that resulted in casualties. Snipers on both sides made it extremely dangerous for any kind of daylight patrolling and machine guns were brought to bear by the enemy on all crossings over the river so that these often were swept by heavy fire at all hours of the night.

Although facing a canal and river over which the bridges had been destroyed by the retreating enemy, it was the purpose of the Fourth French Army to push on after the Huns and force a more extended and less orderly withdrawal along: the entire front. For this purpose the commanding general of the Thirty-sixth was instructed by the commander of the Twenty-first corps to make all necessary reconnaissance, with a view to throwing bridges across the river and canal in this vicinity of Attigny. According to these plans the infantry were to cross the stream either by swimming or other means and establish a bridgehead on the north banks. Covered by the advance of these troops the engineers were to bridge the stream with a structure prepared beforehand and transported to the river under cover of darkness. Over this bridge the supporting troops would pass and be followed by the artillery as soon as sufficient ground could be gained on the north side. Preparatory to the bridging of the stream the Second Engineers, who still remained with the division and who were stationed in the neighborhood of division headquarters at Dricourt, prepared timbers for the bridge and practiced the movements which were expected to be carried out.

With this movement in view efforts were made each night to gather additional information of the enemy across the river. Several patrols were successful to a high degree in spite of the fire from the enemy's machine gunners bearing on the places where crossing was considered favorable. During the night of October 16, patrols from both the 141st and 143d Infantry regiments succeeded in crossing to the north side of the river where they captured two prisoners each and gained valuable information of the enemy troops facing the division. The following night a patrol from the First Battalion of the 142d Infantry, led by First Lieutenant Donald McLennan, battalion scout officer, crossed the canal and river near Attigny and brought back two more prisoners. All of this patrol work was done under the most disagreeable weather conditions. From the time the troops of the division arrived along the river there had been a steady downpour of rain. The men crawled, worked and slept in mud. At Attigny it was possible to cross the canal only by means of a narrow, slippery footlog upon which the enemy's machine guns bore with accuracy. At this point the bridge had been mined and blown up by Russian prisoners of war and they had accomplished their task well.

In addition to his scouts, of the intelligence section. Lieutenant McLennan had volunteers from the four companies of the First Battalion of the 142d, most of whom had sought eagerly for the honor of accompanying the party. While part of the patrol was stationed on the south bank of the canal to cover a hasty retirement in case of necessity, the main portion was led by the scout officer over the slippery log and into the darkness of the underbrush on the other side. Working with the utmost care and making their way slowly and stealthily forward, they passed part of the "boche" wire and obstructions that had been erected between the canal and the river, and then were halted by the sound of low gutteral voices ahead. Here was the chance they had been seeking. Without noise and forgetting much of the possibilities of danger that faced them, members of the patrol started a movement to surround the position from which the sounds had come. So far as could be .fudged by the voices there were only two of the enemy but there might be more. Gradually the patrol closed in from the flanks and then the order came for Fritz to "stick 'em up." One of the two appeared to be a little more than anxious to comply, but the other started to run. Two rifle shots quickly changed the mind of the latter and he also was counted among the prisoners. Realizing that the shots might have attracted a larger German force the patrol was led back to the footlog as quickly as possible. One of the two Germans was inclined to stoutness to a degree that his speed was not keeping pace with that of the patrol leader. In order to assist the rotund prisoner in his progress toward the American lines one of the men employed all the ability he had learned in the use of his feet in a popular American sport and the propulsion of these had the desired effect. The information gained was all that was wanted at headquarters and every member of the patrol was commended for the part he had played in the capture.

After this successful invasion of the enemy's outpost zone every man was keen for a chance to cross the river. Also the snipers did some excellent work. One of these, an Oklahoman, stationed in a post along the canal near Attigny, was credited with at least four successful shots in two days and it was declared that he accomplished other results which could not be verified officially. It grew into a sport not unlike that of hunting big game, this exchange of shots across the river, in which the Americans did all the forcing and had all the best of the argument. The deeds of one sniper were recounted many times over in the regiment afterward. This man chose a position with a sergeant which would enable him to watch for the enemy who were covering the footlog with their rifle and automatic pistol fire. The successful crossings of the canal had made the enemy doubly alert to prevent further effort in this direction. As the sniper and the sergeant lay in waiting the head of a Prussian guardsman appeared cautiously out of a thicket not more than 150 yards away. This was target enough for the sniper who reached over and touched his companion and then squinted through his sights. The crack of the rifle was answered by a convulsive leap on the part of the Hun and a figure clad in field gray lay sprawled on the ground in full view. Both snipers remained at their posts watching for the possible appearance of a second enemy figure and then the man who had fired looked at the other and drawled: "He just kicked once didn't he!"

Where kitchens of front line battalion were stationed between Attiguy and Vaux-Champagne.

With the purpose of effecting a crossing to the north side, constant patrolling was demanded of the troops along the river banks. Day and night these were called upon to cross the canal and ascertain that the enemy had not made an additional withdrawal to the north. At times the observers reported that they could easily distinguish Germans in the back areas out of range of the machine guns and rifles but the demand was made that the troops along the river remain in touch with the enemy day and night in order that any movement to the north might be discovered the instant it began. Responding to these demands from headquarters a volunteer patrol composed of Corporal Allie Gammill and Privates Ted Watrous, Lester Smith and Buster Stinson, all from the 142d Infantry, crossed the canal the morning of October 21. They had been instructed by their commander to secure observation of the enemy on the other side by taking post in the higher buildings of Attigny and vicinity, which they had accomplished from the old sugar mill to the west of the town. Not satisfied with this, however, they had determined to cross the canal and if possible learn something of the enemy in the immediate territory on the north side. Time and again that morning they had been fired upon while near the footlog across the canal. In spite of this they made their way in safety over the precarious footing furnished by the narrow makeshift of a bridge. They had been spurred on by the possibility of capturing three Germans, they had observed while in the sugar mill. But their crossing had been seen. The four were working their way stealthily across the ground between the canal and the river when a burst of machine gun fire brought the patrol leader Corporal Gammill, to the ground. At the same time a group of the enemy was seen making a hurried crossing of the river to cut off the patrol on one flank while the machine gun made it impossible to retreat by the only other avenue of escape. The remaining three of the adventuresome party determined that they would sell their lives as dearly as possible. Armed only with automatic pistols and one rifle they brought a steady fire to bear on the point where the Germans were seen crossing the river. Later it was reported that eight dead Huns lay by the banks of the Aisne at this point. Private Watrous was the next to be hit. In shifting his position he was exposed to the raking fire of a machine gun. In a short time Private Stinson also had been wounded and practically all the ammunition had been exhausted. Realizing that he could be of no assistance to his comrades and that he might be able to carry back important information, the only other man of the party, Private Smith, made a wild dash for liberty and, although there were two bullet holes through his helmet, he plunged into the icy water of the canal and landed safely on the south bank under the protecting fire of his comrades' rifles. The information desired had been secured but at a heavy price and there was little further effort at daylight patrolling.

Where troops of 142d dug in at support position near Vaux-Champagne.

About the same time however one of the scout officers distinguished himself to a degree that he later was given the Distinguished Service Cross. Leading a patrol of several men along the banks of the canal he was caught with his whole party between the cross fire of two German positions on the north side of the river. All secured cover as best they could from some small trees but in a few moments one of the group was wounded severely in the shoulder. There was not sufficient cover to prevent annihilation if they attempted to remain in this position. The officer quickly instructed his men as soon as he had drawn the enemy's fire that all but himself would make their way with the wounded man, around behind the little knoll in front of which they had been caught. Then stepping out into the open he walked backward up the face of the knoll firing his pistol at the enemy. The rest of the patrol quickly made its way to the position of safety and the officer although the target for all enemy weapons bearing on the position, also was unhurt.

Another patrol which secured marked success was conducted across the canal at night by Lieutenant Charles K. Campbell of the 141st Infantry. This patrol lay in hiding throughout the following day and secured valuable information of the enemy from close range, being able to report back to headquarters after darkness with but one slight casualty. It had located five machine gun positions as well as three batteries of artillery. Later the Allied artillery was able to register on these with telling effect.

The Second Artillery Brigade which had remained with the division from the first, was able through unfailing effort to get into position along the river almost as soon as the infantry. In fact the night of the thirteenth the infantrymen had not been able to dig in and prepare their positions for the night before the guns of the artillerymen were making the night hideous with their screeching shells hurled into the "boche" lines. In the support positions at Vaux-Champagne, the infantry was lying in foxholes almost on top of the guns but in spite of the bellowing of the latter at irregular intervals the tired "doughboys" slept soundly until they were called upon to move to another position in the middle of the night. Skillful maneuvering by the artillery enabled the gunners to continue their bombardment constantly with practically no interruption from the enemy's batteries or airplanes. Almost daily the positions of the guns were changed and fire delivered from a different angle than had been the case before. Throughout the engagements the Twelfth Field Artillery had been in support of the Seventy-first Brigade and the Fifteenth Field Artillery had been behind the Seventy-second Brigade. The heavy guns of the Seventeenth Field Artillery had been distributed in the back areas of the division sector as deemed most advisable. During the period of comparative quiet along the river after the Thirty-sixth arrived in position, elements of the Fifteenth Field Artillery were sent to the rear for a short rest, their places being taken by reserve batteries of the Twelfth Field Artillery.

At the time of the division's arrival on the south bank of the river, a message was received at headquarters that a large number of French refugees were collected in the village of Ste. Vaubourg. The division intelligence officer with a chaplain interpreter was sent to investigate the report and found a crowd of men, women and children in a pitiable condition of fright. Due to the fact that these were then in French territory nothing could be done to relieve the situation, other than report it to the commander of the corps. Later however when the village was ordered included in the sector of the division arrangements were made to transport all of the refugees to the rear. In the meantime the town had been covered with white flags. At least one flew from the top of every house. The troops on either side at first had been unable to understand what these meant, but it was noticed that the enemy was excluding the village from his targets on the south side of the river. On the morning that the refugees were transported to the rear however the Hun artillery opened up on them and several casualties were reported. No deaths resulted but the experience added a new episode of horror to the great number that the poor peasants had endured during the four years previous when they had been under the German yoke. Some of the stories told by the refugees were pitiful in the extreme. One woman related her experiences as a cook for German officers on duty at the aviation field. For four years she had not been permitted to secure sufficient funds to get proper clothing for her person and was required to labor under any and all conditions, sick or well.

Wires of all kind, especially in cellars were regarded with suspicion and later when investigation showed that acid had been placed so it would eat through wires set to explode mines in the village of Givry, these suspicions proved to be well founded. A few days after the halt at the river there were several explosions of enemy dumps in the back areas and it is assured that these were set off by time fuses so arranged that they would probably explode when the troops of the Allies had had time to lose suspicion of them. However, all troops had been warned to keep away from these dumps with the result that no one was harmed by the explosions.

Premature plans for throwing a small body of troops across the river as soon as the head of the advance reached the Aisne had been abandoned after reports were received from airplanes to the effect that the enemy had been observed in force to the north of the stream. In the night the patrols could distinguish the sound of shovel? busy with preparing enemy defenses. These reports caused the higher commanders to decide that a movement across the river without considerable preparation, not only would be unsuccessful, but would be attempted only at a heavy loss.

In the days that followed the orders for the division changed rapidly and there was a continual shifting of ground to expand the frontage assigned to it. This acted to forestall any plans that might have been made for crossing of the canal and river. The first of the orders from the corps commander had directed an immediate advance without construction of bridges either for foot troops or for artillery and trains. The French on the right were directed to clean up the river loop to the east of Attigny, at the same time. In the order directing this additional advance, which was issued to be effective October 13, it was announced that the Twelfth French division would be relieved the night of the thirteenth and fourteenth and that the Thirty-sixth Division would be called upon to extend its front to the right in order to maintain the connections in the front line. Orders issued from division headquarters of the Thirty-sixth directed the commanding general of the Seventy-second Brigade to continue the advance across the canal and river and establish his troops in positions on the north bank. At the same time the seventy-first Brigade was directed to take up a position along the river to the east of the Seventy-second Brigade and prepare to push on over the stream as soon as in position. These orders were based on the information received that the enemy was still retiring northward.

When the troops of the Seventy-second Brigade reached the canal they immediately discovered that the north bank was well guarded by German machine gunners, who opened fire as soon as presented with a target. In advancing to the river the brigade suffered two men killed and seventeen wounded and was greeted by frequent bursts of firing from points directly across from Givry. Also the French troops on the right soon discovered that the enemy was strongly intrenched across the neck of land which extended into the loop of the river. Thus it early developed that the crossing could not be accomplished without complete preparation of bridges and strong support from artillery. This particularly was brought out in the later advance of the supporting elements of the brigade. These troops moving up to the front in broad daylight and in plain view came under a concentration of fire that killed twenty-six enlisted men and wounded eight officers and 173 men. This resulted from artillery fire for the most part, although the machine gun fire was heavy.

Airplane observation secured the following day verified the reports from the front line that the enemy still was in force across the river. The activity of the airplanes was most prominent during the period of quiet. The enemy's squadrons outnumbered those of the Allies and they frequently harassed the front and support lines. Often they flew low over the troops burrowing in the ground and spattered the earth with machine gun bullets. During one of these flights the cook of a battalion kitchen just back of the front lines was made the particular object of the airplane's wrath. At the time the captain commanding the regimental supply train was checking up the delivery of rations. The officer and a stuttering cook sought mutual cover under one of the rolling kitchens in which the evening meal was being prepared. Both arrived in position under the firebox of the kitchen at the same time and much after the fashion of a baseball player sliding head first for a base. In a moment or two the captain ejaculated: "Whew, but it's hot!"

"Wh-wh-wh-what's the matter, cap'n, are you b-b-b-b-urinn'?" stuttered the cook.

"You're darn right I'm burning!" exclaimed the captain.

"Wh-wh-wh-why don't you turn over?" solicitously stuttered the cook, and the captain glared his feelings, but presented the other side to be toasted. A little later both emerged perspiring and a little sheepish but happy in the knowledge that the "boche" airmen had flown away.

Responding to the demands of the Twenty-first corps commander that vigorous methods be employed to push forward against the enemy several patrols attempted to cross the river the morning of the fourteenth, but all of these met with stout resistance from the enemy's small arms. One patrol from the 141st Infantry encountered the enemy in the vicinity of the river loop and captured six prisoners and four light machine guns without the loss of a man. It was not until after this effort to cross the river that orders were received that the attempts for a general advance would be abandoned. Instead the troops were directed to make every effort to establish local crossings anywhere possible with a view to placing a bridgehead on the north bank.

Major Hutchings was buried near the place where he fell.

Further shifts in the position were carried out the night of October 18-19, when the Twenty-first Corps headquarters was pulled out of the line and shifted to a position north of Reims. The Thirty-sixth, with the Seventy-third French division, was shifted to the Ninth French corps. Accompanying this information was the additional news that the Seventh French division would be withdrawn from the line the night of October 20-21, and that its sector would be taken over by the Thirty-sixth American and Sixty-first French divisions. The Seventh French division had been on the left of the Thirty-sixth during the entire advance and this change necessitated a shift to the west of the troops in the Seventy-second Brigade. Also the front of the Seventy-first Brigade was widened at least 500 yards near Attigny. In this movement machine guns were so placed that they would cover any gaps that might exist in the widened frontage, all of the front line companies being assigned additional weapons of this character to take care of the added territory.

About this time Colonel John S. Hoover, commanding the 143d Infantry, was relieved of his command at the request of Brigadier General Hulen, commanding the brigade. Command of the regiment passed to Lieutenant-Colonel Irving Phillipson, of the 142d Infantry, who also had assumed command of the 144th Infantry for a few days after the arrival on the south banks of the Aisne, when the colonel of that regiment collapsed and was evacuated to the rear. Later the lieutenant-colonel of the 144th arrived from the hospital and reassumed command. Colonel Jackson of the 141st Infantry collapsed about the same time and was sent to the rear, the regiment being placed in the hands of Lieutenant-Colonel James. Also Major Preston A. Weathered, commanding the 132d Machine Gun Battalion, was evacuated to the rear, the battalion being placed under the command of Captain S. D. Ridings.

Plans were completed for a crossing of the river by the corps October 22, with the Thirty-sixth leading the attack to establish a bridgehead at Attigny. This plan was not favored by General Smith in as much as nothing was to be gained by a crossing of the one division unless the others pushed forward at the same time. However, the corps commander insisted and preparations were completed to this end. They were not to be carried out, however, although they caused the activity of the patrols already mentioned. Detailed plans were drawn and submitted for the establishment of a bridgehead by the Seventy-first Brigade at Attigny, but before the troops could be completely instructed in the details of what was going forward, an order came for the division to shift to the east and take over the greater part of the sector of the Seventy-third French division, which was to be taken out of the line the night of October 22-23. This caused the crossing of the river to be abandoned, but placed the Seventy-first Brigade directly opposite the entire front of the enemy across the neck of the river loop, which was regarded as the most difficult position to be overcome in the push forward.

The new change of position was a side-slip of the entire division, the Seventy-second Brigade turning over part of its sector on the west to the Sixty-first French division. The 142d Infantry was relieved in its entire sector by elements of the 144th Infantry, and then instead of moving over to the east to take over the sector of the 141st Infantry, marched around the rear of that regiment and entered a sector on the east of it, taking over the ground that had been occupied by the troops of the 73d Division. This made the western boundary of the division practically the same that it had been in the beginning, but extended the eastern boundary more than a mile. Under the new arrangements the regiments from east to west in the line along the river were 142d Infantry, 141st Infantry, 144th Infantry and 143d Infantry. This change called for the removal of the Seventy-first Brigade headquarters from Pauvres to Leffincourt, where the brigade reserve troops also were established. All through the night the weary soldiers of the 142d trudged over and through the mud of the back areas to get into position, but the dawn found them at their destinations and ready for further developments that might be undertaken.

These shifts in the position of the troops had meant a constant changing of the lines of communication by the signal battalion, but these managed, by using some of the wires that had been left in position by the enemy, to maintain without interruption telephone and buzzer connections between the command posts of the higher commands and the front line companies. The linemen of the organizations running the wires to the front line companies earned the highest praise by their constant devotion to duty under the most trying circumstances.

About the time the last shift in the line was made there was a noted increase in the amount of artillery fire received from the enemy. In the back areas where the units of supply were called upon to be especially active, the enemy constantly poured his long range fire. In spite of this the ammunition train drove up to the dumps in broad daylight and deposited munitions with impunity. Much of this shelling appeared to be retaliation for an attack by the Sixty-first French Division, which advanced the night of the twenty-fourth and captured the town of Ambly-Fleury. This was a small village on the south bank of the Ardennes canal a short distance to the west of Givry. The French took more than 100 prisoners, among whom were four officers. This was accomplished with practically no losses among the assaulting troops.

Directly after the arrival of the division along the river a field hospital had been set up about two kilometers north of Machault, where all wounded were taken to be evacuated to the rear. The constant occurrence of casualties had caused the division commander to send repeated requests to General Headquarters for replace rents, but only a few arrived, and these were assigned to the 133d Machine Gun Battalion, all the infantry regiments retaining a strength of approximately sixty men to the company, or about one-fourth of the authorized strength. In view of the possible advance across the river, the demand for additional men was vital, but apparently it was not desired to retain the division in this position longer and the desired replacements were withheld.

Chapter Nine - Forest Ferme

Sweeping northeast along the western edge of the Argonne Forest, the Aisne River continues its course until it reaches a point on a parallel with the northernmost edge of that part of the great wood which scatters out northwest of Grand Pre, At this point the river turns sharply to the west until beyond the city of Rethel and then southwest on its course to the sea through Soissons and the Compiegne Forest. At the place where the river turns sharply to the west it is compelled to bend around a high bit of ground that appears unexpectedly from a little flat plain in which nestle the villages of Ste. Vaubourg, Chuffilly, Chardeny, La Roche and Chateau Mery. In curving around this high ground the Aisne makes a decided horseshoe or loop, or which might better be likened to the letter U. The opening of the letter is to the south and the rounded side to the north, as though the letter were inverted. Inside the north end of the letter is the town of Rilly and on the banks of the river about a kilometer to the west of the letter's mouth is the town of Attigny. Across the river from the east side of the loop the ground rises steeply in a series of low hills which are covered with patches of woods and on all sides to the north the terrain quickly reaches an elevation higher than the high ground inside the loop. Snugly ensconced among the ridges of the high ground within the letter is Forest Ferne, hidden from the view of any one approaching until one is almost on top of it, and located a little nearer the western side of the inverted letter U than the eastern side.

Across the opening of the U at the south the Germans had established their line of resistance and had fortified this with a series of wire entanglements cleverly placed so that none of these could be approached without coming in the field of fire of one or more machine guns. These machine guns were placed for the most part in two strong points, one of which was near Forest Ferme and the other and stronger farther to the east in a system of German training trenches, which had been improved and made extremely difficult to attack. Before these strong points there had been placed a double band of wire entanglements, each band being from five to six strands wide and placed low on the ground so that while they might be stepped over; it had to be done with caution in order that the person attempting it would not stumble and fall. These strong points commanded a view of the entire plain to the south, where rested the villages already named, and all around the strong points the enemy had stationed his machine gunners and snipers in such position that each held an excellent field of fire while enjoying perfect cover. In one of these minor positions the Germans were completely hidden by the natural growth of some small brush, while at the same time they were protected by a trench that had been dug partially by rainfall. Here also had been placed minenwerfers of small caliber, as well as light artillery, the latter being somewhat to the rear in the direction of Rilly. The full extent of the German line across the neck of land was approximately two kilometers, or a little less than two miles.

In changing the positions of the various regiments along the Aisne, the regimental command post of the 141st Infantry had not been shifted, although the regiment's front had been moved and extended to the east so that it covered nearly half of the distance across the neck of land. The left of the regiment had been withdrawn from the town of Attigny and placed nearer the brickyard to the east of the town. The eastern part of the German line across the mouth of the loop was faced by the 142d Infantry, which had side-slipped across the area of the 141st Infantry the night of October 22. Headquarters of the 142d had been established in the town of Chardeny, while the command post of the front line battalion had been placed in Chuffilly.

From the time the Seventy-first brigade took up this last position it was under a concentration of fire from the enemy's artillery of all calibers, and was subjected to harassing machine gun fire as well. Possession of the ground within the loop of the river by the Germans meant that the enemy might at his pleasure make a raid upon the American lines or that it might be very favorable ground from which to launch a counter attack at any time. It was these facts that caused the higher commanders to insist that the river loop be cleared, although two unsuccessful attempts had been made by the French a few days earlier.

Both of these attacks had been launched by the troops of the French Seventy-third Division. The first of these, delivered the night of the sixteenth, had been in the nature of an intended surprise attack and had not been preceded by artillery preparation. This had failed completely, the enemy being on the alert and meeting the advance with such heavy machine gun and rifle fire that the assault hardly gained impetus worthy of the name. With a considerable number of casualties the French fell back to their former positions without gaining anything other than the knowledge that the "boche" held the line in great force and that the position would have to be taken with the assistance of strong artillery preparation.

With this artillery preparation the following evening the same troops again advanced to the attack. On the right the assault again was stopped after the assaulting waves had progressed to the second line of wire entanglements. Here the French were met with such heavy grenade, as well as machine gun fire, that they were halted, and when the enemy opened up a heavy concentration of artillery fire in which there was a large amount of gas shell, the right regiment in the assault dropped back to its starting position with heavy casualties. On the left the assaulting regiment was able to progress across a difficult hedge, which ran parallel to the enemy's front near Forest Ferme, but was halted before it reached the actual defenses of the enemy. Here the Frenchmen dug in and remained in spite of counter-attacks which were launched by the enemy the following afternoon. There were two of these counter-attacks, accompanied by heavy artillery barrages, but both attempts to drive the French out of their positions were unsuccessful. During these assaults on the enemy positions at the mouth of the loop, the Allied artillery had concentrated the fire of its heaviest pieces upon the high ground across the river to the east and northeast of the U, but this did not serve to overcome the counter-battery work of the enemy. This is especially interesting in considering the attack of the Seventh-first Brigade against the same loop positions a short time later.

With the changing of the sector and the relief of the Seventy-third French division, came the announcement that for the time being the plan to cross the river at Attigny and attack the Germans on the north banks would be the intention of the high command to clear the enemy from the south bank of the stream and canal before any effort was made to push on beyond, even if a crossing was successful a short distance to the west. With the Germans in the river loop any troops on the north bank of the stream near Attigny would be under a commanding flank fire that would make the ground just to the north of Attigny untenable.

The information that the plan to cross the Aisne had been abandoned was sent out October 23, the day following the change in positions, and at the same time it was announced that the Thirty-sixth Division would be expected to clear the Germans from the south side of the stream on or before October 27. With this announcement also was the information that the division would be relieved from the line the night of October 27-28, and this brought about an unusual situation. It was definitely determined that the Seventy-first Brigade could not prepare completely to make the attack before the twenty-seventh, and that if the troops made the assault at that time they could not be withdrawn that night. This would be extremely inadvisable because of the confusion that would result. Also, if the troops in the support and reserve positions were relieved that night it would place new troops, unfamiliar with the ground, in a position where they would not be able to render the desired assistance in the event of an attack by the enemy in force.

Gen. Pershing saluting the colors at review of 36th Division near Tonnerre.

These matters were presented to the corps commander, General Prax, by Major General Smith, who pointed out at the same time that the positions which would be occupied by the Allied troops within the river loop would be made extremely uncomfortable by the positions held by the enemy in the town of Vonq, and the elevated ground around it on the east side of the river. In addition to these points of vantage held by the enemy it was known that there were strong artillery positions in the vicinity of Attigny, on the north side of the Aisne, which could bring a deadly enfilade fire to bear on the assaulting units. Also General Smith pointed out that if the assaulting battalions were not relieved at the same time the other troops were taken out of the sector, several days would elapse before the command could be reunited properly. In turn the corps commander explained that the possession of the ground to the south of the Aisne by the enemy was preventing the successful attack of the French forces to the east, who were preparing to advance against the Germans and force them to retire still farther northward. General Prax also promised that the assault battalions would be relieved the night following the departure of the balance of the division, and that these battalions would be transported to the rear to the vicinity of Somme-Py by French camions instead of marching like the other troops. He explained that the French troops who would relieve the assault regiments were seasoned soldiers and were familiar with the sector, having been given detailed information of the conditions and having made a study of the terrain. He also explained that these would be in readiness to move forward promptly in the event of a serious demonstration by the enemy as a counter movement and besides that all American dead would be taken care of properly, their graves marked and interment conducted with fitting ceremonies.

In this manner it finally was settled upon that the division would clear the enemy from his positions in the loop and the Seventy-first brigade was selected to make the attack. The commanding general of the Seventy-first Brigade was directed to draw up his plan of operations along certain lines laid down by the division commander and when this was submitted it was approved immediately. It called for the attack to be made with the two infantry regiments abreast, the 142d on the right and the 141st on the left, each with one battalion in the assaulting waves, one battalion in support and one battalion in the brigade reserve at Leffincourt. The 131st Machine Gun Battalion was placed with the supporting troops near Chardeny. The Third Battalion of the 142d Infantry was selected to conduct the assault with the Second Battalion in support, the First Battalion just having been relieved from the front line positions when the regiment was side-slipped from before Attigny. In the 141st Infantry the troops of the First and Second Battalions were combined for the attack while the other battalion was stationed in the vicinity of Leffincourt as part of the brigade reserve. With the assaulting troops were Companies B and C of the 132d Machine Gun Battalion as well as a group of trained wire cutters from the Second Engineers, whose task would be the cutting of wire that might interfere with the advance. Each of the regiments supplied a group of infantrymen accompanied by machine guns to conduct liaison on the right and left and protect any gaps that might occur in the line where the regiments joined during the assault. The exact hour for the attack to commence was not known until the day of the twenty-seventh when it was received by the men after they actually were in position.

Preparatory to the assault the artillery of the Second Division was to prepare with a standing barrage of twenty minutes on the "boche" positions, pulverizing them, and then a rolling barrage was to move forward at the rate of 100 yards every three minutes. The attacking infantry was to begin the move forward with the start of the rolling barrage and to follow this as closely as possible in order not to allow the enemy to emerge from his dugouts and begin firing before the attacking infantry was upon him. In addition the commander of the corps artillery was placed at the disposal of General Smith with elements of his artillery which were to register their fire on the positions of the enemy across the river and in the back areas of the neck of land to be taken. The Second Trench Mortar Battery of the Second American Division also was brought into position to pour demolition fire upon the front line positions occupied by the "boche."

To further assist in the attack the corps commander had designated that the Czecho-Slovak brigade of the French division on the right, assist in the attack by furnishing liaison with the right of the Seventy-first Brigade. The personnel of this brigade was made up for the most part of Poles from the United States, all of whom spoke English and the stories related by all of them as to how they managed to get to Europe were extremely interesting. No less than three of them in the liaison group acting with the 142d Infantry explained that they had been turned down repeatedly when they tried to enter various branches of the United States Army, one because he was married, another because his eyes were not good and still another because he could not read and write the English language.

Preparatory to the attack the advance command post of the 141st Infantry was moved up to the town of Ste. Vaubourg. The headquarters of the 142d Infantry remained at Chardeny. The troops of both regiments suffered severely from the enemy's artillery fire during the days of preparation and waiting before the attack. The greater part of the shells which came over was laden with gas, the mustard shells predominating. The concentration of this fire in the vicinity of Chuffilly, where one shell registered a direct hit on the command post of the Third Battalion, 142d Infantry, that the troops around the town were burned by the splashing liquid in the fox-holes where they lay. They were moved back to the positions near Chardeny until the evening before the attack in order that they might be protected from the gas bombardment, although the effect of the poison was negligible except where the liquid itself splashed on the victim before it had time to be vaporized into gas and dissipated by the atmosphere.

During this bombardment the division gas officer paid a visit to the area and declared that it was dangerous for troops to be there. Most of the men in the front line and support positions however had become well acquainted with the danger of the location by that time and although a move was made to the positions farther to the rear, there was much deriding the idea that gas could be made extremely dangerous in the open.

The plan of attack for the twenty-seventh called for the general advance to be made to a line just beyond Forest Ferme where the positions taken were to be consolidated, and for patrols to push on forward to the town of Rilly on the banks of the canal. These patrols were to exploit the ground thoroughly in order that no Germans might remain south of the river uncaptured, and that preparations might progress that would enable the troops to advance across the river at this point,

A high state of morale existed in all ranks. The men had gained confidence in their ability, that had come with experience under fire. In the darkness of the early morning October 27, the assaulting echelons crept into their positions before the German wire and concealed themselves to lie in waiting through the greater part of the day before the signal for the attack would be given. Here they were so well camouflaged that the enemy was not aware of their presence at any time before the assault and then did not know it because those in position to see either were driven into their dugouts or were killed by the American artillery barrage.

The hour set for the attack to begin was 16:30 o'clock, French time, or 4:30 p.m. American time. It was well selected, as at that hour the visibility was so poor, the enemy on the heights across the river could not observe what was taking place, while the attacking forces still had sufficient light to see their way clearly and to make no mistakes. To assist in overcoming the visibility and observation afforded the enemy, a smoke screen was prepared and placed in such a manner that it completely hid the advancing infantry from the machine gunners across the river and prevented them from firing on the positions in the loop even after these were captured.

The signal for the assault was the firing of a lone piece of artillery. This marked the start of the preparatory bombardment on the enemy's positions. This lone cannon broke the stillness of the late afternoon and the waiting doughboys crouched in their positions knew the fight was on. For twenty minutes the bursting shells from the Allied pieces dropped a curtain of high explosives on the trenches and fox-holes occupied by the enemy. Apparently unable to discern what was taking place the enemy artillery response to this fire was weak, only a comparatively small volume of fire falling on the positions occupied by the troops waiting for the beginning of the advance. Patiently the men rested with their weapons in position, while officers leading companies and platoons watched the slow movement of the watch hands creeping around to "H hour", the time set for the movement to begin. The artillery beat upon the earth in front as steadily as the rolling of a drum while the smoke screen drifted over the enemy positions and between the objectives and the enemy positions across the river so that lack of observation practically eliminated machine gun fire from that direction.

Then as the moment arrived for the barrage to roll forward, up out of their places rose the waiting infantrymen. Slowly and steadily they pressed onward up the slope toward the two strong points, one at Forest Ferme and the other in the little wood to the east. They were following the barrage so closely that they were almost "leaning against it." Everything was orderly. They were veterans now. Whereas all had been uncertainty and confusion before St. Etienne, everything was orderly and precise now.

The first belt of wire was reached and crossed. Some of the men stepped over while others walked through without difficulty where the strands either had been severed by the artillery fire or were cut by the engineers, who accompanied the advance. Much of the wire remained intact, but little heed was paid to this. There was no defense by machine guns and rifles, the "boche" remaining crouched in his positions of shelter and unable to get out. The artillery was still beating upon the front line positions. Still advancing as steadily as at parade the first waves reached the second belt of wire. Again they clambered over and through. Here and there a man was falling but these were few. The intervals between men in the assaulting waves were large and the enemy's shells were having little effect. The second belt of wire was passed.

Bayonets ready the advancing infantry jumped into the trenches of the enemy before the Huns could emerge from their places of shelter. Some of these were met as they attempted to come out of their dugouts. In almost every case their hands immediately shot into the air and the cry "kamerad" was squealed before there was a chance for action. Position after position was overcome in this manner, the front line not hesitating to clean up the captured ground, leaving that to the special details of men picked for that purpose and which were coming closely behind. Without a halt the advance was continued until the final objective was reached and then while the barrage was held and allowed to play steadily on the areas beyond for thirty minutes the infantrymen with picks and shovels dug places of shelter along the captured line and prepared to defend it against possible counter attacks. But none was to develop. As the assault reached its final objective a German messenger dashed out of the entrance to a dugout and attempted to escape in the direction of Rilly. Quickly a member of the intelligence section leveled a shotgun and brought down the fleeing Hun. The German was not wounded seriously and declared that although he had been in the fighting throughout the war it was the first time he had been wounded. He was found to be carrying important dispatches and was a valuable capture.

Beginning the assault the 141st Infantry had been withdrawn slightly in order that the men in the first waves would not be so close to the barrage that they would come within the range of the bursting shells. During the early morning of the twenty-seventh the assault troops of this regiment had been withdrawn slightly to a jumping-off trench and there they lay in waiting throughout the day. A few minutes before the hour for the advance to begin, the enemy's counter barrage began to fall but it was placed so that all of the shells fell in rear of the assault troops and practically no casualties resulted from this. The riflemen and automatic riflemen in the two assault waves had little opportunity to use their weapons. They were upon the Germans before the latter had a chance to attempt a defensive. The bombers however were busy tossing their explosives into the dugouts and making sure that none of the enemy was hiding, until such time as they might operate their weapons in rear of the assaulting troops. In a few instances German machine gunners attempted to get their weapons into action but were silenced immediately. On two occasions the men cleaning up the dugouts captured more than twice their number of prisoners. The total casualties of the regiment was only twelve. One of these was Lieutenant Charles M. Ford, who was killed by a bursting shell. Two enlisted men also were killed by shell fire and the nine other casualties were wounded.

In the preparations of the 142d Infantry for the attack a novel scheme of keeping the movements of the troops secret was worked out. The entire country was covered by a network of abandoned German wires which were suspected of having been left purposely in such a condition that the enemy across the river could connect up with them and "listen in" to the messages being transmitted to various parts of the American lines. More than once there had been evidence to indicate that such things were being accomplished. To overcome this condition Colonel Bloor selected some of the most intelligent Indians from Company E, composed almost entirely of redmen from Oklahoma, and stationed them at the telephones. These Indians were members of the Choctaw tribe and when the written messages were handed to them in English they transmitted them in their own tongue and it is reasonably assured that no word of this was picked up by the Huns.

Instructed at an assembly of the officers of the regiment the leaders of the 142d Infantry troops took station early on the morning of the twenty-seventh with the single line that lay camouflaged directly under the forward German positions. There they remained until the hour for them to start the advance when they rose and moved steadily forward. The bursting shells of the enemy's counter-barrage fell directly among their ranks and shells of the friendly barrage falling short of the enemy positions also fell among them. For a few moments there was confusion but for a few moments only. Quickly the ranks were reorganized and moved onward. When the Germans rushed from their dugouts as the barrage moved forward, they found the 142d Infantrymen waiting for them with rifles, grenades and trench knives in their hands. The Huns barely had time to realize what was happening before they were prisoners. The recovery of the Infantry after being fired upon by their own artillery, and meeting the heavy fire of the enemy's guns at the same time, was made the subject of the highest praise both by the French and the American commanders.

The machine gun company of the 142d Infantry was attached to the 132d Machine Gun Battalion for the operation and assisted the gunners of that organization in putting down the machine gun barrage ahead of the advancing troops. These guns sprayed every yard of the positions occupied by the enemy, and other guns of the battalion accompanied the advancing infantry to be placed in positions such that would enable them to sweep the front with fire in the event of a counter-attack, while the captured ground was being consolidated for the defense. The battalion suffered five casualties in the action, all being enlisted men who were wounded by shell fire.

The casualties of the 142d Infantry were heavier than either of the other two organizations engaged in the assault. Eight men were killed on the field and sixteen wounded. Most of these occurred during the time the troops came under the combined fire of the friendly artillery and the enemy's guns. All of the losses were among the enlisted men.

Refugees from devastated northern France and their traveling home.

As soon as the final objective had been reached along the line running east to west through Forest Ferme, strong patrols were pushed out to clear up the entire area of the river loop, including the town of Rilly at the northernmost extremity of the neck of land. In this cleaning-up movement none of the enemy was found. If there had been any in the areas back of the front line positions they had retreated across the river.

The attack on Forest Ferme resulted in the complete destruction of the Prussian Guard battalion stationed in the loop. This battalion was from the Ninth regiment of the Third Prussian Guard division, reputed to be one of the best in the German army. After the close of the action it was found that the prisoners numbered four officers, five non-commissioned officers and 185 privates. The dead counted on the field was only slightly less than this number. So far as could be ascertained every other officer and man of the battalion, including the commanding officer and an artillery officer attached for duty, was killed. The prisoners were much better in appearance than those captured during the action before St. Etienne. The Germans around Forest

Ferme were well clothed, cleanly shaven and apparently were well supplied with tobacco and food.

In addition to the prisoners taken the brigade captured thirty-one machine guns, a large quantity of rifles, grenades, mortars and trench stores. The general appearance of the stores and their arrangement indicated that the enemy had expected to maintain his position on the south side of the river indefinitely.

During the assault there had been a demonstration with artillery in the vicinity of Attigny to distract the attention of the enemy from the real attack. That this was successful in a measure was indicated by several heavy explosions across the river from Attigny. Following the attack fires were reported in the enemy lines during the night. These were in the vicinity of Voncq and Semuy and demonstrated the expectation of the enemy that the Allies would attempt a crossing of the river in that vicinity in the immediate future.

For the operation against the river loop the Seventy-second Brigade had retained only one infantry regiment in position, the 144th. The mission of this regiment was only to remain in position on the left flank in readiness to participate at any time it might be called upon to repel any counter movement of the enemy near Attigny. The 143d Infantry already had been relieved, and withdrawn from the sector. This occurred the night of the twenty-sixth when the French took over the positions held by that regiment, and the 144th Infantry was withdrawn the following night.

The assault on the enemy positions within the river loop had been carried out in every instance as prescribed by the field orders of the commanders. Not a detail was neglected. The discipline, the liaison, the following of the barrage and the development of the position after it was taken were accomplished just as laid down in the books of tactics, and the whole operation took on the aspects of a maneuver. The effect of the trench mortar fire on the enemy positions before the advance was noted with particular interest by the observers on the hills to the rear, where every move made by the assaulting waves could be seen. Unlike the former operations of the brigade, there had been time to inform all ranks of the plans for the attack so that every soldier as well as officer knew what was to be done. Thus in spite of the darkness that fell soon after the close of the assault, the men went about establishing the line on the exact positions prescribed in the sketches that had been provided previously. The effective aid of the Second Engineers who assisted in destroying the wire in the path of the infantry was highly commended by the troop commanders.

The assault battalions were retained in the positions they had captured until the morning of October 29, when they were marched to the rear and then transported in camions to rejoin their regiments. The support battalions in each regiment were sent to the rear the night of the twenty-eighth, being taken as far south as Somme-Py in camions. The front line positions were all taken over by the French before daylight of the twenty-ninth, at which time all troops of the division had passed out of the firing zone to the rear. The front line battalions were transported in camions to a point near Camp Montpelier, a French rest camp in the vicinity of Somme-Suippe, which point also was reached the evening of October 29 by the balance of the division. The troops relieved from the line the night of October 27, had been bivouacked in the vicinity of Machault until daybreak when they had continued to march to Somme-Py. There they camped for the night. The march from Somme-Py to Camp Montpelier had consumed all of the following day. Division headquarters had been set up at Camp Montpelier and from there directions were given out for the billeting of the troops and the distribution of supplies.

When the sector had been turned over to the French, the German prisoners that had been used to clean up the rear areas were turned over also. Ammunition and supply dumps had been cleaned up and the material at these had been transported to the railhead. Field hospitals that had been set up near the front line to take care of the wounded in the last engagement, were taken down hurriedly and transported to the rear and the division passed from the zone of actual fighting for the balance of the war, although nothing of the kind was indicated at the time.

Of great interest to the men during the day following the attack on the river loop had been the efforts of the German airplanes to scatter propaganda. Many pamphlets printed in French and English had been dropped on the front line area. These pointed out that a new form of government was being set up in Germany, that the fourteen points of President Wilson had been accepted and that hostilities were to stop soon. The question was asked why the useless fighting should continue. This crude effort to lower the morale of the Allies was met with much jesting.

As if to retaliate for the clean cut manner in which the Americans had wiped out the German battalion within the loop, the enemy's batteries concentrated their fire on this part of the line during the night and day following. Guns of all calibers played on the back as well as the forward areas. The loss of the positions was a serious handicap to the enemy. From the vantage points in the captured territory the Allies constantly threatened the German lines to the east and permitted the farther advance of the French forces in that direction. Also it enabled the artillery to bear on important German communication points so that the lines of supply were interrupted. The Seventy-first Brigade again had come out of the fighting with great credit and had earned a record for aggressiveness that might well be envied by older and more experienced organizations.

Chapter Ten - To Bar-Le-Duc — the Armistice

Although Camp Montpelier was far from attractive in appearance, being little more than a collection of great barns and half dugouts covered with frame roofs and walls that projected from three to four feet out of the ground, yet it represented the first buildings that the troops had been able to sleep in for a month. After the mud and rain that had been their daily lot along the Aisne the shelter of the wooden structures was more than welcome. Little or no straw was to be had but by this time the men had learned to take care of themselves. From the neighboring pine trees they secured enough needles to make beds and in some of the buildings fires were started.

Probably the most welcome of all things afforded at Camp Montpelier for the officers was the change of underclothing that was secured from the baggage which had been left at Suippes and Somme-Suippe. As soon as the troops had been placed in billets and assured of the evening meal, wagons were sent to the dumps where the baggage had been placed and this was brought to the camp. Not all of the officers were fortunate enough to find their things and many of the bedding rolls and bags had been rifled of their most important contents, but most everybody was able to appear the following morning in clean clothing for the first time in many weeks. The enlisted men were not so fortunate as a rule. Their packs had been brought up to the river after having been dumped at Somme-Py, just before the actual front line had been entered but much of the clothing had been stolen by passing troops until but few of the real owners of the property ever received the things belonging to them. In this manner many things belonging to the dead, which would ordinarily have been sent back to the relatives in the United States, disappeared never to be found.

The march from the front to the Suippes area had been a trying ordeal for many who had become weakened from long exposure. Again the improved roads had to be avoided in order that the long trains of supplies and ammunition for the troops in the front line might not be blocked. There had not been the forced onward pushing that had characterized the entrance into the lines because there was not the same demand for speed and there was more time for the men to look about them. On the way back over the battlefield around St. Etienne most of the organizations found time to halt and permit the men to look at various points where comrades had been killed and to clear up hazy impressions that existed about the lay of the land during the fighting. There had been a few solemn moments at the burial places to the southeast of the village, where those who had fallen had been gathered together and grouped according to regiments.

Then the march had been continued south of Somme-Py over the old Hindenburg defenses. The path once more led through the mazes of barbed wire where the ground was strewn with "dud" projectiles that were avoided with the greatest care. These projectiles were being exploded as rapidly as possible by German prisoners, while here and there a French sentry stood guard at the entrance of a dugout to warn others that explosives had been piled therein to be set off as soon as the preparations were complete. Many of the shells scattered about on the ground were almost the size of a small man, being the largest projectiles fired from the German naval guns.

After this march from the lines there was general expectation that the troops would be allowed to rest in the vicinity of Suippes, but rumors to this effect proved to be erroneous. During the night of the twenty-ninth billeting officers were roused from their beds and sent away in trucks and automobiles to prepare places for the troops to rest the following night, and with the dawn came orders for all units to be on the road and marching eastward by 8 o'clock. By this time orders had been received transferring the Thirty-sixth Division from the Fourth French Army to the First American Army, then engaged in the bitter struggle for the possession of the Argonne territory between the Meuse and the Aisne Rivers.

The night of the thirtieth the division was billeted in the area just to the west of Ste. Menehould, on the ground where the forces of Frederick the Great had met reverses at Valmy. The troops of the 142d Infantry were billeted in the town of Valmy itself and the following morning marched over the hill where the French had made their victorious stand against the forces of the famous. Prussian general. During the day previous the march had been conducted parallel to the old front line affording the columns of men additional opportunities to observe the ground where the French had made their one big successful drive against the Germans in 1915,

From the area west of Ste. Menehould the division continued the march southeastward toward the Triaucourt area, division headquarters being established in the town of Dampierre the night of October 31, where it remained until the morning of November 2, the troops having stopped in this area one day to rest. They had been on the march since the night of October 27, and although there had been but few cases of exhaustion many of the men showed the effect of the long tramps on the hard roads. Some were lame and sore from ill-fitting shoes, which were all right on the soft ground but which chafed while marching on the highways.

The morning of November 2, the march again was begun and the head of the leading column entered the edge of the lower Argonne Forest. That night the troops were billeted in the villages around Triaucourt itself, but the final move had not been made. Sunday, November 3, the columns were on the road again at an early hour and some of the troops exceeded thirty-five kilometers before the final halt was made. Throughout the day the reports of the guns at the front could be heard with more distinctness than had been the case since the area around Suippes had been left. In the early morning the columns had passed through the lower edge of the Argonne wood and then headed almost due south. By night the most advanced columns were in the vicinity of Bar-le-Duc.

In this area the entire division was directed to remain until replacements could be received and some much needed equipment could be secured and distributed. Division headquarters was established at Conde en Barrois, a small town about twenty miles slightly south of due west from the town of St. Mihiel and about thirty miles almost due south of Verdun.

Two days were given the troops to rest from their long marches and settle themselves in their billets as well as mend and wash their clothing, which had been long neglected. At the end of that time it was announced that every energy would be directed toward getting back into condition to enter the lines again in the final push to break through the German defenses. The area in which the division was billeted had just been abandoned by the First Division, American Expeditionary Forces, which had rested there after its first entrance into the Argonne struggle, and which had just marched away to the north to engage in the final fighting of the war in the vicinity of Mouzon and Sedan. Even as the Thirty-sixth was making its last march on the third the Fifth Corps under Major General Charles P. Summerall was breaking through the last defenses of the Kriemhilde Stellung and forcing the retreat of the Huns in the direction of Sedan.

General view of cemetery from the southeast, about 2500 "Good Dutchmen" buried here.

At the end of two days in the area north of Bar-le-Duc the division began to receive replacements and a strenuous program of training was prescribed. Lessons that had been learned under actual fighting conditions were remembered and combined with the theories that had been instilled with the instruction before the lines were entered. Daily the troops were taken to improvised ranges and given special instruction in the use of the automatic rifle, as well as the automatic pistol and grenades. Special attention was directed toward the use of the pistol, a weapon with which the men had not been armed in the first training period around Bar-sur-Aube. Cold rains were the rule, but these were not considered. From early morning until late at night the troops were in the field getting ready for the time when they again would engage the enemy in battle.

While at the front division headquarters had been kept informed daily of the progress of the fighting in the Argonne as well as in the other theaters of operations. The fall of Lille and other places in Flanders and Belgium had been proclaimed and the newspapers had told of the collapse of Turkey and Bulgaria. In the Triaucourt area the papers published in Paris were distributed daily through the division area by the representatives of the Y. M. C. A. and other organizations, and all of these indicated that the end was near. Still there was no let-up in the efforts to get the division in shape for the expected movement into the line again in the near future. Most of the replacements were from the Thirty-fourth Division, made up of the National Guard from Nebraska, South Dakota and Iowa, splendid soldiers who had been through long periods of training at Camp Cody, New Mexico, and who had been made replacement troops as soon as they landed in France. Others were casuals from the hospitals or who had been picked up by the military police while absent without leave from their organizations. These last named however were few indeed. Some of the old men who had been wounded in the fighting around St. Etienne were among those who came from the hospitals and there were several officers and non-commissioned officers who had been at the First Corps School at Gondrecourt, while the division was in the line. These were among the most eager to get the men in shape for another try at the Hun. They had missed the other fighting and were keen to get a chance under fire.

Insufficient replacements were received to bring the organizations up to full strength but most of the infantry companies were given enough men to make a strength of approximately 200 men, which, was more than most of them had been able to enter the line with the first of October. Due to the fact that most of these were trained soldiers great confidence was added to the organizations and with the experience in the Champagne it was assured that the division would take care of itself if ever brought against the enemy again. Most of the men were re-equipped completely with clothing, the old uniforms being placed in a salvage dump and hauled away after the fresh clothing had been issued. Additional arms and equipment also were distributed and after several days of training the personnel began to look forward with anticipation to another meeting with the enemy.

This however was not to be. The morning of November 7, the news was received that the German government had asked for an armistice and that representatives of the government were on their way to France to treat for terms. Among the peasantry these things were not considered as being probable. Wherever it was mentioned the French people gravely shook their heads and explained that they had been at war more than four years and that the news was too good to be true. However when the fact of the armistice finally was announced colors of France, as well as the other nations represented among the Allies, sprang into existence to be displayed in the houses everywhere. Most of the troops of the division were at drill the morning the final news of the cessation of hostilities came. During the early part of the morning the bombardment at the front had been more distinct than had been the case prior to that date. As the clock pointed first to 10 o'clock and then toward 11 o'clock the firing grew in volume until the men began to wonder if the enemy had turned and was delivering an unexpected counterblow at the Allied lines. Then suddenly the bombardment ceased and all was quiet. It was at this time that the message sent by radio from Eiffel Tower at Paris was received. Everywhere the news was published there was a demonstration. The men danced and sang and shouted themselves hoarse. All wrote letters home and began to count the days when they would be returning to the United States.

But the training program was to be continued. Although the armistice had been arranged and plans were in progress for the occupation of Germany it was considered likely that there might be further need for fighting men and in order to maintain the troops at the highest possible point of efficiency there was a daily routine of maneuvers against machine gun positions, practice in scouting and patrolling and combat practice on the range. This work was doubly hard after the cessation of hostilities however. While there had been a prospect of using their knowledge against the enemy the men were willing to go through any hardship to accomplish the desired results, but with this prospect gone the work and exercises soon grew uninteresting and irksome.

Therefore when an order came for the division to move to the area around Tonnerre, a small city on the main highway between Paris, Dijon. Lyon, Marseilles and Nice and about 100 miles from Paris, there was general rejoicing. The move was made by marching and proved the longest of the kind ever conducted by the division. The troops started the morning of November 18, and did not reach their destination until Thanksgiving. On the way to Tonnerre they passed through the Thirteenth training area around Bar-sur-Aube, where they were greeted joyously by the French people with whom they had lived while training before entering the fight. In every French home dinner was prepared for as many guests as could be accommodated and wine of many years vintage was brought out of the cellars to celebrate the occasion.

On the march from the area north of Bar-le-Duc to the Sixteenth Training Area around Tonnerre the division was transferred from the Seventh Army Corps to the First Army Corps, commanded by Major General William M. Wright, with headquarters at Tonnerre itself. The headquarters of the Thirty-sixth was established at Cheney, a small town about nine kilometers northwest from Tonnerre on the highway to Paris and the division was billeted in the surrounding towns. South and east of Tonnerre the Seventy-ninth and Eightieth Divisions, also a part of the Corps were billeted. During the march from the north there had been keen competition between the regiments of infantry to see which could establish the best record. In this the honors went to the 142d Infantry which had the smallest number of men to fall out from exhaustion yet which remained in the van of the movement and reached its billets in the Tonnerre area ahead of all others. The entire division concluded the march in the best of health and with the men in fine physical condition.

Part of the 36th division waiting to pass before Gen. Pershing in review near Tonnerre, France, March 9. 1919.

Chapter Eleven - Operations of the 111th Engineers

On the march to the Tonnerre area the division once more was joined by the 111th Engineers who had been marched away from the training area around Bar-sur-Aube, September 10, to participate in the operation against the St. Mihiel salient. Companies A and E of the 111th Supply Train also returned to the division just prior to the movement from the Triaucourt area after having been on detached service with the First Army troops in the vicinity of Verdun during the closing days of the fighting.

From their billets near Bar-sur-Aube the regiment of engineers had been transported by rail to the town of Frouard just north of the city of Nancy and near the juncture of the Moselle and Meurthe Rivers. This was along the eastern side of the St. Mihiel salient and directly south of Pont-a-Mousson, one of the best known sectors to American troops in the entire war. The night of September 12. when the attack against the salient had progressed to such a point that it was already proclaimed the greatest possible success, the regiment moved up to Gezoncourt and the following night to Martincourt.

just north of the old positions in that sector of the American troops so often referred to in the early days of 1918 as the "sector northwest of Toul."

The next day the engineers were given their first experience of building roads under artillery fire. During the two preceding days they had been within hearing of the big guns as they roared their defiance at each other. They started to work on the roads at Regnieville the morning of September 14, and for the next three days there was hardly time for meals as they struggled to make the road across the old French and German defenses passable for the heavy traffic that was demanded. As at all other places where the lines of the opposing forces had remained stationary for four years there was a strip of ground about four miles wide that had been blown to powder as the battling armies had burrowed beneath the surface or plowed up the ground with their enormous shells and mines. The whole surface of the earth in this strip was pulverized stone and gravel mixed with broken munitions and rubbish. All signs of former roads had disappeared and a complete new highway had to be constructed in order that the heavy artillery might move forward with the infantry in the attack

In the construction of this highway the engineers displayed an ability that earned them the praise of the army commander. They were cited in orders for their excellent work and no regiment of engineers in the army did better work of this character. At the time they were serving as corps engineers for the first corps and during the time they were employed in the St. Mihiel drive they constructed more than five kilometers of road, or a complete highway between Regnieville and Triaucourt. Until this task was completed the men worked night and day. They were separated into three detachments and the way for the heavy traffic was prepared with amazing rapidity. The entire construction had been accomplished in less than five days.

At the conclusion of the road building between Regnieville and Triaucourt the regiment was allowed to rest one day and then started on a march across the rear of the American forces at the front, with its destination in the vicinity of the Argonne Forest. During the next six days and nights the road builders were moving westward. The daylight marches soon were abandoned. The troops rested during the day and marched at night in order to avoid observation from the enemy. This was brought about largely due to the fact that while passing through the town of Blenod the enemy had secured observation that enabled him to bring a concentration on the entire column including the trains. Poor marksmanship however left the engineers little the worse for this, only three men being wounded and none killed.

At the end of the period of marching the regiment established headquarters at Camp Beaudelle, in the Argonne wood near Les Islettes a few miles west of Clermont. This was September 22, four days before the beginning of the general assault by the First American Army between the Meuse and the Aisne and which has been referred to generally as the battle of the Argonne. The camp at Les Islettes was in the heart of the Argonne Forest proper. During the next two days the regiment moved to Boureuilles and Vauquois, two small towns just to the south of Varennes, made famous as the city in which Louis XVI and Marie Antoinette were intercepted in their flight to safety during the French revolution. This was around the point known as Hill 260 and the regiment arrived in position in time to follow up the assault that had driven the Germans back from the old line and started the long battle that was to end only with the capture of Sedan and the declaration of the armistice.

Here again the work of constructing roads while the ground was being shelled by the heaviest guns of the enemy was the task assigned the 111th and again good fortune favored them. Although other units in the same vicinity, notably the 110th Engineers of the Thirty-fifth Division, suffered heavy casualties, only a few of the men from the Thirty-sixth were hit. Company D, organized at Tulsa, Oklahoma, had the distinction of going through the entire campaign without a casualty. While working around Hill 260 a giant German shell came over and exploding in the midst of a group working on the roads almost wiped out a whole platoon of the 110th Engineers but failed to harm any of the personnel of the 111th. About the same time a Captain of the 111th Engineers was eating his lunch when an enemy airplane came over and sprayed the ground with bullets. One of these dashed the officers mess kit from his hand but failed to touch his person.

From the vicinity of Varennes the regiment worked its way northward behind various combat divisions, passing through Apremont, Sommerance, St. Juvin, St. Georges, Imecourt, Sivry, Buzancy, St. Pierremont, Oches and Le Besace to Raucourt, only a short distance south of Sedan. As in the operation against the St. Mihiel salient the regiment was divided into three detachments and in the latter part of the drive against Sedan was enabled to keep up with the advance of the infantry only by dint of the most strenuous marching as well as incessant labors to keep the roads in condition for the advance of the artillery.

The engineers were in position at Raucourt November 11 when the armistice was signed and immediately turned their faces southward out of the line for the first time since their entry into it before the St. Mihiel attack. As corps engineers they had been called upon to do only road construction and at no time had been sent into the front line positions as frequently had been the case with division engineers, but often they were under fire of the enemy's artillery and were made the targets for enemy bombing squadrons as well as "boche" airplanes armed with machine guns.

In the advance from south of Varennes to the final objective south of Sedan they had been in close touch with some of the most famous fighting of the war. The assault of the Thirty-fifth Division from the initial point in the drive to Charpentry and beyond, the desperate drive of the First Division over the defenses of Hill 240, Hill 272 and through the German defenses to the Kriemhilde Stellung, the smashing of that famous line by the Fifth Corps and later the record breaking marches and assaults against Mouzon and Sedan, all took place immediately in front of the engineers. Probably no other organization in the army was in closer touch with these great battles than the regiment of road builders from Oklahoma and Texas.

In the advance the men were called upon to construct all kinds of roads. Most of the work had to be of a temporary nature, especially in the latter stages of the fighting when the greatest pressure was being brought to bear to keep the artillery up with the infantry. In addition to the construction of the roads the engineers were called upon to assist the military police in the regulation of traffic, designating which roads could be used by heavily laden trucks and which were suitable for the passage of heavy artillery.

In connection with the work of building roads the regiment accomplished a task that again won for it the praise of the army chiefs. Taking over the corduroy road which formed a detour of a quarter mile around the main highway at Briulles, the regiment was directed to rebuild with plank the main highway which had been destroyed by heavy shelling. The minimum space of time was set for the construction of the road by the chief engineer of the corps but the men set to work with such a will that in addition to making endless repairs on the corduroy road they completed their task forty-five minutes ahead of the limit set by the chief engineer.

During its whole tour of duty at the front, covering two months under fire the 111th Engineers lost only one man killed and nine wounded. The number of men sick in the hospital also was correspondingly small, probably the most exceptional record of any organization engaged in similar duty in the army.

Gen. Pershing decorating the colors of 36th division.

Arriving in the Tonnerre area about the same time as the infantry the engineers again were assigned the task of keeping up the roads in the Sixteenth Training Area and throughout the winter had their hands full. The heavy trucks hauling supplies to all parts of the area soon cut the roads so badly that they were almost impassable in places and it was necessary to augment the forces of engineers with details from the infantry. At the front the roads had been maintained by the use of stone taken from demolished houses in the villages but this could not be done in the Tonnerre area where it was necessary to blast rock from the quarries and haul it over great distances to the point:; where it was needed most.

Due to the fact that there were few casualties in the regiment there were few changes in the personnel of the officers, most of those who went to Europe with the command remained with it and returned to the United States in the same capacities that they had occupied in going over.

Chapter Twelve - Home Again

Hardships were the rule when the Thirty-sixth Division first arrived in the Tonnerre area. As a usual thing the billets provided for the enlisted men were of the poorest character, beds often being on the ground and many being quartered in stables. Just prior to the departure from the Triaucourt area a large number of casuals had been assigned to the division and these had not reached their organizations until the march had begun. Most of these men were not completely equipped and under the bad conditions that existed at first in the Tonnerre area they suffered severely. By hard work and excellent supervision, however, most of the poor conditions were overcome within the course of two months. Billets were cleaned thoroughly and beds were constructed by the use of planks and wire netting. Stoves were improvised and continual labor prevented the mud from becoming impassable for supply trucks.

The greatest shortage was in shoes, many of the men having become almost barefoot from long marching on the hard roads. In some cases it became necessary to relieve these men from all duty until they could be supplied with new shoes. This was done during the month of December when additional clothing was also supplied. At no time was there sufficient wood for the demands of the command. Most of the men and officers were compelled to secure additional fuel besides that issued by the supply department. Fortunately the winter was mild as compared to the winters preceding and the health of the command was excellent at all times. It continued to grow better month after month until during April only about nine men out of every thousand were carried on the sick reports and most of these were suffering from minor ills. Other divisions suffered severely from influenza during the winter but in the Thirty-sixth there were only 160 cases. In addition to these there were 111 cases of pneumonia and thirteen cases of meningitis, causing five deaths. The rate of venereal disease in the division was remarkably low. It was less than half the rate recorded in the examination of men for military service in the states of Texas and Oklahoma during the war and was more than a third less than the rate for the entire American Expeditionary Forces. The deaths from all diseases during the stay in the Tonnerre area was about three men per thousand as compared to the death rate of fifteen per thousand in the United States. This high state of health was due to the close supervision of sanitation by all officers from the division commander down to the lieutenants commanding platoons. The men were required to take baths regularly by roster and a system of examinations and inspections prevented any illness from existing more than a day without becoming known to the surgeons.

Athletes established an enviable record during the winter. The division football team composed of players for the most part from the colleges of Texas and Oklahoma, but which was headed by Captain Wilmot Whitney, Harvard, fought its way to the final game at Paris before it was defeated. It won the championship of the First Army Corps by defeating the teams from the Seventy-ninth Division, Eightieth Division and First Corps Troops, in turn. Then it won the championship of the First Army by defeating the crack eleven from the Twenty-ninth Division, champions of the Fifth Corps. The Seventh Division team, champion of the Second Army was the next team to be defeated, being overcome at Bar-sur-Aube in a game which was watched by General Pershing, King Albert and Queen Elizabeth of Belgium, Lieutenant General Hunter Liggett and Lieutenant General Robert L. Bullard as well as other notables. The final battle was staged at Prince Park in Paris where the Eighty-ninth Division team, champions of the Third Army, was encountered. In a clean but hard-fought game the Eighty-ninth Division team won by a score of 14 to 6, and probably the most bitter part of the defeat was the fact that Lindsay, one of the half backs of the winning team, was the chief ground gainer for the victors and lived in Oklahoma.

In military framing the men of the division also established their superiority. During a military tournament, or fete, at Tonnerre, March 15, the teams representing the division won every decision but two in ten events and so far outclassed their opponents in most of the events that there was little competition. These competitions included rifle and pistol firing, wall scaling, bayonet fighting, signalling and various other feats necessary to the proper training of efficient soldiers. In this competition the platoon from Company A, 142d Infantry, was declared to be one of the most proficient in close order drill ever exhibited by the army. All of the organizations of the First Army Corps were represented in the tournament.

Later in the spring the First Battalion of the 143d Infantry after gaining the right to represent the division in a maneuver competition, won first place in the corps competition and second place in the maneuver competitions held by the army.

Besides the football competitions, basketball and baseball games were played throughout the spring. Each regiment and many smaller units had organized baseball teams and each company had a basketball team.

Schools were established in every town in the area and the work of organizing these was pushed to such an extent that thousands of men were afforded their first opportunities for studying mathematics as well as the more advanced courses of study in English and history. These schools were taught by officers and competent enlisted men and served to enable many of the men to occupy their evenings when otherwise time would have hung heavily on their hands.

Recreation also was developed in every possible way. Besides the troupes of entertainers brought into the area by the Y. M. C. A. and other organizations the various companies formed small theatrical troupes and toured the division area. Some of the regiments, notably the 142d Infantry organized splendid companies of entertainers. The 142d Infantry troupe later was adopted by the division and placed on the circuit for the entire A E. F. It gave a performance in Paris before the division sailed for the United States.

Early in December, leaves were granted for officers and men and these continued to be issued throughout the winter and spring until every man in the division had been given an opportunity to visit Southern France, Italy or England. The greater number of officers as well as men visited the Riviera along the Mediterranean and at some time nearly every member of the division had an opportunity to go to Paris. More than 2,000 visited the French capital to see the final football game and each week during the late spring a number of leaves to Paris were granted.

The conduct of the officers and men in the leave areas in the south of France caused the highest commendation from the officers in charge of the areas. The enlisted men were taken to and from the areas in special trains and were furnished with lodging while at the leave areas. The records of the division showed that about 18,000 officers and men were permitted to go on leave during the spring and winter and that reports of misconduct were made against only eighteen of these. Most of these reports were of such a minor nature as not to be considered and the only one of a serious character was never proved.

In addition to the schools conducted by the division itself, the schools and universities of both France and England were offered to many officers and men. These were taken advantage of to the fullest extent, especially those offering courses in languages and the arts and sciences.

Without warning the Commander in Chief visited and inspected the division March 9. The entire command was assembled a short distance north of Tonnerre and marched in review. Prior to the review General Pershing inspected every rank and file of the assembled forces and decorated several officers and men with the Distinguished Service Cross. At the same time he decorated the colors of the various organizations in the division with the battle streamers earned at the front. The ribbons on the flags bear the inscription: "Meuse-Argonne Offensive (Champagne Sector)". Addressing the assembled officers and soldiers at the close of the review the general spoke of the splendid manner in which they had borne themselves at the front in spite of the fact that they had not been afforded the usual preparation in a quiet sector, that had been given to most of the divisions. He urged them to maintain the high state of discipline and morale that had been observed in the past and return to the United States with a record of which they might remain proud through the balance of time.

After his departure from the area General Pershing expressed his appreciation for the fine appearance of the division and its showing against the enemy in the following letter to the division commander:

"My dear General Smith: —

It was with great pleasure that on April 9th, I inspected and reviewed the 36th Division north of Tonnerre. In noting the splendid physical condition of its personnel, I could well see why your combat record in France, though short compared with some others, is one of which all ranks may well be proud.

"Arriving in Europe toward the end of July, the 36th Division was at once sent to an area near Bar-sur-Aube, where for two months it followed the regular course of training which had been prepared. In October, however, as the great Allied attack was nearing a crisis, it was thrown directly into the active battle without the usual preliminary month's training in a quiet sector of the line. In this emergency the division responded to every call made upon it. With the veteran 2d Division it operated under the Fourth French Army in its drive west of the Argonne, which was made in conjunction with the Meuse-Argonne attack of the First United States Army. The 71st Brigade on October 8th, attacked from St. Etienne-a-Arnes. On the 11th the entire division was in and advanced in the next two days approximately twenty-one kilometers to the Aisne River. Continuous contact was kept with the enemy while preparations were made for crossing the Aisne. No further advance, however, was made, although on October 27th, the troops of the 71st Brigade attacked and captured Forest Farm. The Division was relieved October 29th.

"The bearing of the Division in this, its first experience in battle, showed the mettle of officers and men, and gave promise of what it would become as a veteran. Please, therefore, extend my congratulations to the members of your Division, who may return home proud of the record of their services, with the knowledge that they have acquitted themselves well as part of the American Expeditionary Forces.

"Very sincerely yours,

JOHN J. PERSHING,
General, Commander in Chief,
Am. E. F."

Relations between the personnel of the division and the populace of the French towns in which they were billeted, were the most cordial. In some instances there was friction caused by the misunderstandings of both, but in view of the difference in languages and temperament these may be said to be extremely few. The French language was learned rapidly by officers and men and there were many occasions when the troops were entertained in the homes of the French people. Evidence of these relations is best given by the fact that one officer and eight enlisted men of the division carried French brides home with them when the command finally departed. During the spring there was a series of farewell dances given by the various organizations of the division to which a great many French civilians, men and women were invited.

In the Tonnerre area the officers and men of the division found many interesting places to visit. Near the headquarters of the Seventy-first Infantry Brigade, located in the town of Flogny, was an old Roman camp that had been occupied by the troops of the Caesars when they garrisoned various places in France from 500 to 800 A. D. and the chateau occupied by Brigadier General Pegram Whitworth and his staff was the site of one of the most famous castles in central France. Souvenir hunters among the soldiers of the 142d Infantry dug up a quantity of old Roman coins in the Roman cemetery near the camp. In nearly every village in the area the churches afforded matters of the greatest interest to students of religious history, some of the buildings being very distinctive of architectural periods. At Tanlay, where the Seventy-second Brigade headquarters was located there was a castle surrounded by a moat filled with water and this was an unceasing object of interest to the soldiers billeted in the area. Tonnerre itself abounded in interesting places, one of which was a great spring that sent forth a volume of water two feet in diameter.

As soon as the troops had become comfortably situated in their billets once more a schedule of training was carried out. The new men received during the march from the Triaucourt area had to be taken through a course of instruction to determine what places they were to fill in each company and similar organization and every phase of military training was taken up. For many months after the division reached the Sixteenth Training Area there was no intimation that it would be sent home until practically all of the troops in Europe had been shipped back to the United States. From time to time orders were published setting forth the dates upon which various divisions would go to Le Mans and from there to the port of embarkation but the name of the Thirty-sixth appeared in none of these lists. Resulting from this it was rumored that the division would be sent to the Army of Occupation in Germany to relieve one of the divisions of drafted men on duty there but there proved to be no foundation for this. During the course of training there was a complete schedule of instruction with the rifle, the automatic rifle and the machine gun. Ranges for extensive firing with the rifle were not available on account of the nature of the terrain, which was flat and afforded no hills into which the riflemen might direct their bullets in order to prevent them from doing harm. There were maneuvers of all kinds however, including several in which the entire division was engaged and numerous contests were conducted to keep alive the interest of the men.

While the infantry and other branches of the division in the Tonnerre area were going through this course of training the Sixty-first Field Artillery Brigade was being prepared at Camp de Coetquidan for return to the United States. Orders for the brigade to turn in all equipment and animals to the various depots of supply and countermanding the orders to join the division, were issued. Inspections, preparatory to the return trip across the Atlantic became the routine work.

The last football game at Paris, 36th and 89th divisions playing at Prince Park.

Brigadier General Stephens who had been in command of the brigade from the time it left the United States for France, became ill with pneumonia the latter part of December and died January 4, at the hospital at Camp de Coetquidan. He was buried in the camp cemetery with military honors befitting his rank and in the presence of high officials of the French army. The funeral oration was delivered by Lieutenant General d'Amade, commanding the Tenth Region, French army, in which he paid eloquent tribute to General Stephens as being representative of the fine body of American artillery officers sent abroad by the United States. Command of the brigade was assumed by Colonel F. A. Logan, of the 133d Field Artillery, until sometime in February when he was relieved by Colonel Otho W. B. Farr of the regular army. The brigade was reviewed by General Pershing, February 23, and a week later the movement to the ports of embarkation was begun. The regiments of the brigade were together for the last time at Camp de Coetquidan. Each was transported by rail to St. Nazaire and from there they sailed to Newport News, Va. From Newport News the 131st Field Artillery was sent to Camp Travis, near San Antonio, Texas, for demobilization while the 132d and 133d regiments were sent to Camp Bowie.

There were few changes in the personnel of the artillery brigade officers during the stay in Europe. Some were transferred to other branches of activity immediately before the brigade was shipped back to the United States but the great majority of the personnel returned home with the troops and were demobilized at the same time. Colonel Logan alone of the colonels remained in the service temporarily as demobilization officers at Camp Bowie.

Without warning the commanding general of the Thirty-sixth also received order to prepare and move to the Le Mans area, preparatory to going home. This order was sent by telegraph April 10, and was out of a clear sky, no intimation having been given from General Headquarters up to that time that the division would be sent home before the middle of the summer. The command was delivered into the hands of the Service of Supply April 15, when the work of turning over all properties was begun and within a few days reports were made that all organizations were ready to entrain. The advance party started for the Le Mans area April 26, and the division as a whole arrived there during the first few days of May.

Again in the LeMans area the division established an enviable reputation for discipline, preparedness and ability to take care of itself at all times. The inspectors' reports forwarded to the Commander in Chief showed that the division was in the highest state of preparation for returning home and the orders issued by the division commander for the inspection were forwarded as a model for other divisions passing through the area. The inspectors declared that no other division of all those returning home had made a better showing than the Texans and Oklahomans. The men presented a splendid appearance, all of them wearing the shoulder insignia of the division and having their clothes fitted properly. The insignia was an arrowhead of blue upon which was superimposed the letter "T," all on a circular disk of khaki. The "T" also was of khaki, and represented the Texas contingent of the division while the arrow head represented the Oklahomans. This insignia had been adopted while the division was in the area north of Bar-le-Duc immediately after signing of the armistice when all divisions in the Expeditionary Forces were directed to submit designs for approval at G. H. Q.

The first contingents of the division to start for Brest and from there to the United States left Le Mans the morning of May 17, and within a few days all had arrived at the port and were placed on board the transports with an average wait of three days. Again at Brest the various units were required to go through the delousing process which already had been conducted at Le Mans and with more or less frequency in the Tonnerre area. Also additional equipment and clothing was issued at Brest where it was needed. Before leaving the Tonnerre area a large number of officers had been ordered to join the Army of Occupation in Germany and during the stay at Le Mans still other officers were assigned to duty in France, some going to Tours and others to various places of activity in the Service of Supply.

Just before the sailing of division headquarters the following letter of farewell was delivered by the Republic of France through its representative at Brest:

"FRENCH REPUBLIC
Paris, May 19th, 1919.

"French Premier
Minister of War

"From: The French President, Minister for War.
"To: Commanding General, 36th Division, U. S.

"My dear General:
I am so happy to extend to the 36th Division U. S., when it is going to leave France, the cordial greeting of the Government of the Republic.

"Your division arrived in France at the time when the great battle was in progress which was to decide the fate of the war. It took a glorious part in it. The fighting which it did from the 8th of October, and which led to the Aisne, between Attigny and Givry, proved the valor and the spirit of discipline of your soldiers.

"I send them my affectionate wishes at the time when they go back to their homes. I wish that the remembrances of their Campaign in France remain lively in their hearts. France will not forget the generous help which they brought to her.

"Believe, my dear General, in the assurance of my very devoted feelings.

For the Premier,
and by his order,

The General Commission for Franco-American War Affairs

(Signed) ANDRE TARDIEU."

On the return trip to the United States heavy seas were encountered and two men of the 142d Infantry, on board the cruiser Denver, were washed overboard and drowned. These were Corporal Harry S. Hovey of Company E, and Private Joseph C. Strong of Company H. Otherwise the voyage was pleasant for all. Instead of crossing the ocean in convoy as had been the case before, each transport set out for itself and arrived at different harbors in the east. The 142d Infantry debarked at Boston, the 143d Infantry at Newport News, from which place it also had embarked for Europe, while the balance of the division landed at Hoboken. All were taken to the camps adjacent to the ports preparatory to shipment to the demobilization points and once more required to pass through the delousing system. Replacements who had joined the division in France and who lived in other parts of the country were separated from their organizations at the camps in the east and bade goodbye.

Typical billet in France after the Armistice. This was the stable of a chateau.

Just before going aboard ship to embark for Galveston instead of going overland by rail, the 141st Infantry was discovered to have several men afflicted with smallpox and the organization was placed in quarantine at Camp Mills for seventeen days. The balance of the division was taken by rail to Camp Bowie for demobilization, several of the organizations parading at various points in Oklahoma and Texas on the way to Fort Worth. At all of these places they were received with ovations, particularly in Oklahoma City where the 142d Infantry marched through the streets.

As rapidly as possible men and officers were mustered out of the service at Camp Bowie and allowed to return to their homes. Most of the officers accepted leaves of absence for fifteen days in order that they might adjust themselves to the conditions in civil life, but a few remained in the service temporarily on recruiting duty for the army.

Although in the line facing the enemy but a comparatively short time the division had earned an enviable record overseas. In its assault against the "boche" around St. Etienne and its subsequent advance of twenty-one kilometers to the Aisne River, the news dispatches of the world declared that it had "taken a glorious part in the world's history." In its fighting it had captured three pieces of heavy artillery, six pieces of light artillery, four howitzers, 17 trench mortars and 277 machine guns besides small arms such as rifles and pistols in great quantities. It is estimated that the amount of munitions and material captured by the advance to the Aisne was valued at $10,000,000 or more. Certainly it was reported that the German supply of gas shells captured at Mont St. Reny was the largest that ever fell into the hands of the Allies. Every kind of warfare was experienced by the troops and in all they performed with credit. It had captured prisoners each time that prisoners were asked for by the higher commanders. No troops could have behaved with better morale under the worst possible conditions and while the division might have suffered less losses with more experienced leadership and more intimate knowledge of conditions at the front, yet it accomplished the tasks assigned to it and accomplished them well. It suffered twenty-three officers and 486 men killed, sixty-four officers and 1,450 men wounded, thirty-five officers and 427 men gassed and eighty men missing. The greater number of these losses were in the Seventy-first brigade which bore the brunt of the fighting.

For the valor of the division personnel in action two medals of honor, thirty-nine Distinguished Service Crosses, one Distinguished Service Medal, and a great number of French decorations were awarded to the officers and men. Major General Smith was made a Commander of the French Legion of Honor while four other officers were decorated as Chevaliers of the Legion of Honor. Seven men were decorated with the Medaille Militaire, the highest award for enlisted men in the French army, while 415 officers and men were decorated with the Croix de Guerre.

How the division behaved under its ordeal before a desperately fighting enemy is best told in the message of General Naulin, commanding the Twenty-first Corps of the Fourth French Army at the time the Thirty-sixth first went into action:

"The 36th Division, U.S., recently organized, and still not fully equipped, received during the night of 6th-7th October, the orders to relieve under conditions particularly delicate, the Second Division, to drive out the enemy from the heights to the north of St. Etienne-a-Arnes, and to push him back to the Aisne.

"Although under fire for the first time, the young soldiers of General Smith, rivaling in push and tenacity with the older and valiant regiments of General Lejeune, accomplished their mission fully. All can be proud of the work done. To all, the General Commanding the Army Corps, is happy to express his cordial appreciation, gratitude and best wishes for future successes. The past is an assurance of the future.

(Signed) GENERAL NAULIN."

The Honor Roll

Killed in Action

OFFICERS

141st Infantry

ALCORN, L. C. 2d Lieut., Co. K.....October 8, 1918
BURCHILL, JOSEPH M., 2d Lieut., Co. M.....October 8, 1918
COX, AUBREY W., 2d Lieut., Co. K.....October 9, 1918
DREW, WALTER W., 2d Lieut., Co. K.....October 9, 1918
FORD, CHARLES M., 1st Lieut., Co. D.....October 28, 1918
HUTCHINGS, EDWIN G., Major, ___.....October 8, 1918
KENDRICK, HUGO O., Captain, Co. K.....October 9, 1918
LUHN, GRAHAM B., 1st Lieut., Co. D.....October 8, 1918
McKINNEY, JOHN C, 2d Lieut., Co. L.....October 8, 1918
MORRISON, CLYDE T., 1st Lieut., Co. E.....October 8, 1918
OGDEN, IRA C. Captain, Co. F.....October 10, 1918
WEHNER, CARL, 2nd Lieut., Co. K.....October 9, 1918
WRIGHT, BENJAMIN F., Major.....October 8, 1918

142d Infantry

CARRIGAN, ALFRED N., JR., 1st Lieut., Co. L......October 8, 1918
COLLINS, THOMAS F., 2d Lieut., B.....October 8, 1918
GOEBEL, GEORGE. 2d Lieut., Co. M.....October 8, 1918
HANNER, CARTER C. Captain, Co. E.....October 8, 1918
HANSON. DAVID T., Captain, Med. Det.....October 8, 1918
HARRISON. RICHARD. 1st Lieut., Co. F.....October 8, 1918
HORNKE, EMIL C, 2nd Lieut., Co. H.....October 9, 1918
LOWERY, KEITH, 1st Lieut., Co. C.....October 10, 1918
MATHENY, ARTHUR J., 1st Lieut., Co. B.....October 8, 1918
PEARCE, WILLIS L., Captain, Co. F.....October 8, 1918

132d Machine Gun Battalion

CROUCH, HUTT, 2d Lieut., Co. C.....October 8, 1918

141st Infantry

BROWN, ARTHUR S., 1st Lieut., Med. Det.....October 9, 1918
AKINS. SAMUEL E., Private, Co. C.....October 8, 1918
ALLEN, ELZA F., Private, Co. C.....October 8, 1918
ALLEN, JESSE J., Private, Co. B.....October 8, 1918

ALLEN, OTHOM R., Private, Co. G.....October 8, 1918
ANDERSON, FRANK. Private, Co. C.....October 8, 1918
ANDEKSON, THEODORE, Private, Co. C.....October 8, 1918
ANTONIO, ARES G., Private, Co. A.....October 8, 1918
AKERS, JOHN B., Private, Co, F.....October 8, 1918
ARMSTRONG, HUEY C., Private, Co. B.....October 8, 1918
ARNOLD, JACK, Corporal, Co. D.....October 8, 1918
ATCHISON, CLAUDE, Private, Co, C.....October 10, 1918
BAILEY, ABE M., Private, Co. C.....October 8, 1918
BAILEY, EARL S., Private, Co. C.....October 8, 1918
BAILEY, EDGAR A., Private, Co. C.....October 8, 1918
BAKER, EDDIE A., Corporal, Co. L.....October 8, 1918
BARBER, REUBEN, Private, Co. C.....October 8, 1918
BAIRD, CLARENCE A., Private, Co. D.....October 8, 1918
BARNARD, JOHN, Mechanic, Co. D.....October 8, 1918
BAYLOR, JOHN R., Sergeant, Co. C.....October 8, 1918
BEDFORD, ARTHUR, Private, Co. B.....October 9, 1918
BELL. IVAN A., Private, Co. K.....October 8, 1918
BENNETT, ANDREW E., Private, Co. C.....October 8, 1918
BIGDEN, GEORGE E., Sergeant, Co. B.....October 8, 1918
BIRDWELL, WILL M., Private, Co. K.....October 9, 1918
BLAGKBURN, PETER R., Private, Co. C.....October 8, 1918
BLANCHETT, FRANK C., Private, Co. C.....October 8, 1918
BOLD, ADAM, 1st Sergeant, Co, B.....October 9, 1918
BOOKER, W. E., Private, Co. E.....October 8, 1918
BOYD. JESSE J., Private, Co. C.....October 8. 1918
BRINKROFF, EDMUND, Private, Co. C.....October 8, 1918
BROWN, WILLIAM W., Corporal, Co. D.....October 8, 1918
BURNS, HARRISON B., Private, Co. K.....October 8, 1918
BUSSEY, JOHN T., Private, Co. A.....October 8, 1918
BLACKMORE. JESSE D., Private, Co. D.....October 8, 1918
CAMPBELL, CLYDE. Private, Co. D.....October 8, 1918
CAMPBELL, WILLIAM, Private, Co. E.....October 8, 1918
CARILE, HICK R., Private 1 cl., Co. C.....October 8, 1918
CARLILE, JAMES W., Corporal, Co. C.....October 8, 1918
CARTER. JOHN T., Private 1 cl., Co. C.....October 8, 1918
CHANDLER. ESPER F., Private 1 cl., Co. C.....October 8, 1918
CHOATE, JASPER D., Private, Co. B.....October 9, 1918
CLANCY, WILMER, Private, Co. A.....October 9, 1918
CLICK, TERREL A., Private, Co. D.....October 8, 1918
COLLINS, JIM C., Private, Co. A.....October 9, 1918
CORREN, JACK. Corporal, Co. B.....October 8, 1918
COX, MARTIN V., Corporal, Co.....October 7, 1918
CRADDOCK, THOMAS D., Corporal, Co. D.....October 8, 1918

DAVENPORT, JOSEPH B., Private, Co. M.....October 8, 1918
DAVENPORT, ROBERT, Private, Co. B.....October 9, 1918
DeARMON, WAYNE, Private, Co. A.....October 8, 1918
DENNIS, HOMER H., Private, Co. B.....October 8, 1918
DITZLER, FRANK H., Private, Co. A.....October 8, 1918
DOAKE, THOMAS M., Private, Co. B.....October 8, 1918
DOGGET, MOHON, Corporal, Co. B.....October 9, 1918
DOMSTAD, ALBERT. Private, Co. M.....October 8, 1918
DOOLEY, THOMAS M., Private, Co. B.....October 9, 1918
DORNAK, STEVE. E., Private, Co. L.....October 8, 1918
DUKE, WALTER E., Private, Co. B.....October 8, 1918
DULIN, L. A., Private, Co. E.....October 8, 1918
DUNLAP, JOHN C., Private, Co. I.....October 9, 1918
DUNN, JOSEPH C., Private, Co. B.....October 8, 1918
DURHAM, BARTLETT C., Private, Co. B.....October 9, 1918
DUSTON, JAMES E., Private, Co. B.....October 9, 1918
ELLIS, N. M., Private, Co. E.....October 8, 1918
ENGLISH, ROBERT I., Private, Co. B.....October 9, 1918
EVANS, CLYDE, Corporal, Co. B.....October 8, 1918
EVERETT, JOE W., Private, Co. B.....October 8, 1918
ELLIOTT, MARVIN, Private, Co. C.....October 8, 1918
FARMER, CARROLL, Private, Co. A.....October 9, 1918
FERGUSON, W. C., Private, Co. E.....October 8, 1918
FIELDKAMP, H. J., Private, Co. E.....October 8, 1918
FISHER, ALBERT W., Private, Co. B.....October 9, 1918
FRAUSTE, FRANK, Private, Co. E.....October 8, 1918
FRAZIER, JOHN A., Private, Co. F.....October 9, 1918
GARCIA, FRANCISCO, Private, Hq.....October 7, 1918
GASTON, ROBERT A., Corporal, Co. F.....October 8, 1918
GREEN, H. P., Private, Co. E.....October 8, 1918
GREEN, TROY E., Private, Co. B.....October 8, 1918
HABY, OSCAR J., Private 1 cl., Co. C.....October 8, 1918
HALL, JOHN, Private, Co. F.....October 27, 1918
HANCOCK. VERNER, Private, Co. F.....October 9, 1918
HARRIS. PHIL P., Private, Co. K.....October 8, 1918
HEATH, LESLIE L., Corporal, Co. K.....October 8, 1918
HILL, JOHN T., Private, Co. B.....October 9, 1918
HILDEBRAND, B. W. C., Corporal, Co. E.....October 8, 1918
HORNER, JOHN B., Corporal, Co. H.....October 8, 1918
HOUSTON, P. C., Corporal, Co. B.....October 9, 1918
HOWELL, THEODORE J., Corporal, Co. D.....October 9, 1918
HEWETH, PEARL, Private, Co. I.....October 9, 1918
HUMPHREYS, CALVIN, Private 1 cl., Co. C....October
HUMPHREYS, WILLIAM, Sergeant, Co. C....October 1918
HURT, F. J., Private, Co. E.....October 8, 1918

JOHNSON, JESSE S., Private, Co. I.....October 7, 1918
KESSELER, OTTO, Private, Co. M.-G.....October 8, 1918
KILLOUGH, W. L., Corporal, Co. E.....October 8. 1918
KING, VANCE A., Corporal, Co. B.....October 9, 1918
KITCHENS, CLARENCE, Private, Co. M.....October 8, 1918
KOCH, JOHN L. Private, Co. G.....October 17, 1918
LANDRUM, WILLIE, Private, Co. D.....October 8, 1918
LAWRENCE, JOHN P., Private, Co. C.....October 8, 1918
LAWSON, W. E., Private, Co. E.....October 8, 1918
LAYNE, WILLIAM S., Private, Co. D.....October 8, 1918
LEIBER, OSCAR J., Private 1 cl., Co. C.....October 8, 1918
LEONARD, DENNIS E., Private, Co. D.....October 8, 1918
LEONARD, TIMOTHY, Private, Co. C.....October 8, 1918
LERO, JOE F., Corporal, Co. B.....October 8, 1918
LESTER, BEN. Private, Co. B.....October 8, 1918
LINE, LIGE, Private, Co. K.....October 8, 1918
LUTZ, ERIC T., Private 1 cl., Co. C.....October 8, 1918
LYNCH, FRED D., Private, Hq.....October 8, 1918
MAEHR, CARL F., Corporal, Co. D.....October 8, 1918
MALONE, LON F., Private 1 cl., Co. C.....October 8, 1918
MARTIN, ROBER A., Private, Co. I.....October 7, 1918
MAYO, MARION, Private, Co. C.....October 8, 1918
McCLOUD, EMMET. Private, Co. D.....October 8, 1918
McDERMOTT, CALIP F., Corporal, Co. D.....October 9, 1918
McFARLANE, HARRY A., Private, Co. D.....October 8, 1918
McGINNIS, RUSSELL R., Private 1 cl., Co. C.....October 8, 1918
McKNIGHT, Cornelius R., Private, Co. D....October 27, 1918
MEYER, HUGO W., Private, Co. I.....October 10, 1918
MILLER, LAWRENCE, Corporal, Co. C.....October 8, 1918
MITCHELL, LAWRENCE I., Private, Hq.....October 8, 1918
MORRE, JOHNNIE, Private, Co. G ....October 8, 1918
MORGAN, LYMAN, Private, Co. K.....October 8, 1918
McBURNETT, WESLIE, Private, Co. K.....October 8, 1918
NETHERY, ALBERT C, Private, Co. F.....October 9, 1918
HOFIRE, ANDY. Private, Co. D.....October 9, 1918
NORMAN. JOHN B., Private, Hq.....October 8, 1918
OAKLEY, STEPHEN R., Private, Co. D.....October 8, 1918
PAGE, WARREN B., Private, Co. F.....October 9, 1918
PARMER, WILLIAM E., Private, Co. I.....October 9, 1918
PELECH, JOE, Private, Co. C.....October 8, 1918
PERKINS, OVERTON, Corporal, Co. B.....October 27, 1918
PERRYMAN, HOMER W., Private, Co. C.....October 8, 1918
PERRYMAN, WASHINGTON L., Private, Co. K.....October 8, 1918
PINDER, T. E., Sergeant, Co. E.....October 8, 1918
PITTS, DOUTHITT, Private 1 cl., Co. C.....October 8, 1018

POERNER, AUGUST, Private, Co. C.....October 8, 1918
POLVADE, ERNEST, Private 1 cl., Co. C.....October 8, 1918
PRINCE, J. E., Private, Co. E.....October 8, 1918
RAINS, CURTIS A., Private, Co. D.....October 8, 1918
ROGERS, HERMAN, Corporal, Co. E.....October 8, 1918
ROUMELITIS, DIEMICIOS, Corporal, Co. C.....October 8, 1918
REDDING, BENJAMIN, Private, Co. I.....October 9, 1918
SAVAGE, REMMIE, Corporal, Co. D.....October 8, 1918
SCOTT, GEORGE R., Sergeant, Co. A.....October 8, 1918
SELF, GEORGE W., Private, Co. H.....October 9, 1918
SHERRED, THOMAS J., Private, Hq.....October 8, 1918
SIMMONS, CONNIE, Private, Co. I.....October 9, 1918
SMITH, ISAAC, R., Corporal, Co. L.....October 8, 1918
SMITH, T. R., Private, Co. E.....October 8, 1918
SMITH, THOMAS E., Private, Co. L.....October 22, 1918
SPEEGLS, GILES, Sergeant, Co. K.....October 8, 1918
STEVENSON, HARRY L., Private, Med. Det.....October 8, 1918
STORM, IRA D., Private, Co. F.....October 9, 1918
TARR, CHARLES L., Private, Co. D.....October 8, 1918
TERRY, BRYN, Private 1 cl., Co. G.....October 12, 1918
THOMPSON, MARENUS, Corporal, Co. D.....October 8, 1918
TREVINE, ALEJERANDRO G., Private, Hq.....October 8, 1918
TEUCCI, GUISEPPE, Private, Co. D.....October 8, 1918
TURNER, J. W., Mechanic, Co. E.....October 8. 1918
VADEN, ROBERT, Sergeant, Co. M.....October 7, 1918
WALKER, ROY D., Private, Co. M.....October 8, 1918
WALKER. CLYDE J., Corporal, Co. C.....October 8, 1918
WARD, SAMSON, Private, Co. K.....October 8, 1918
WALTERS. CHARLES, Corporal, Co. B.....October 8, 1918
WARE, GUS B., Corporal, Co. C.....October 8, 1918
WATSON. TOM B., Private, Co. B.....October 8, 1918
WEISS, JOSEPH W., Corporal, Co. C.....October 8, 1918
WELCH, JESSE L., Private, Co. I.....October 8, 1918
WHITE, WILLIAM A., Private, Co. D.....October 9, 1918
WILLIAMS. ALVIN J., Private, Co. K.....October 8, 1918
WILLIS. PAUL. Sergeant, Co. K.....October 8. 1918
WOLLOM, OLE S., Private, Co. M-G.....October 8, 1918
WOOD, HORACE U., Private, Co. M.....October 8, 1918
WOODUL, CHARLES E., Sergeant, Co. B.....October 8, 1918
WOODS, RUFUS C., Corporal, Co. I.....October 8, 1918
WRIGHT, ADOLPH K., Sergeant, Co. I.....October 9, 1918
YEARY, JOHN N., Corporal, Hq.....October 8, 1918
YECHIS, MICHAEL, Private, Co. I.....October 9, 1918
ZUERCHER, L. L., Corporal, Co. E.....October 8, 1918
ZERNICKE, JOHN, Private, Co. I.....October 9, 1918

142d Infantry

ADAMS, JAMES E., Private, Co. F.....October 9, 1918
ADAMS, MARVIN L., Sergeant, Co. F.....October 9, 1918
ADAMSON, WESLIE H., Private, Co. H.....October 8, 1918
ALLEN, PHILLIPS S., Private 1 cl., Co. B.....October 8, 1918
ALVERSON, GARRY L., Sergeant, Co. D.....October 9, 1918
ALVEY, FLOYD G., Private 1 cl., Co. L.....October 8, 1918
ARNALL, ROY. J., Private, Co. G.....October 8, 1918
BAIRD, CHARLES W., Private, Hq.....October 9, 1918
BANNER, ROBERT F., Private, Hq.....October 9, 1918
BLAND, THOMAS C, Private, Co. H.....October 8, 1918
BLANKS, JAMES L., Private, Co. H.....October 8, 1918
BOONE, JESSE M. S., Private, Co. G.....October 8, 1918
BOUSE, CHARLES S., Sergeant, Co. B.....October 9, 1918
BROWN, ALFRED N., Private, Co. K.....October 27, 1918
BROWN, ARTIE E., Private, Co. F.....October 9, 1918
BROWN, NICHOLAS E., Corporal, Co. E.....October 8, 1918
BURCH, WALDO. Private, Co. B.....October 9, 1918
BUTLER, FREDDIE A., Mechanic. Co. M.....October 9, 1918
BURNETT, ARLEIGH. Sergeant, Co. B.....October 9, 1918
BYERLEY, EARL C, Sergeant, Co. G.....October 8, 1918
CALVERT, OLLIE S., Sergeant, Co. M.....October 9, 1918
CAMPBELL, CHESTER F., Private, Co. L.....October 8, 1918
CAMPBELL, HIRAM W., Private, Co. L.....October 8, 1918
CARPENTER, QUINCY C., Bugler, Co. G.....October 8, 1918
CARR, BOB, Private, Co. F.....October 9, 1918
CHILDRESS, AMOS R., Corporal, Co. K.....October 9, 1918
COBB, BRUCE, Corporal, Co. K.....October 27, 1918
CLARK, AUBYN E., 1st Sergeant, Co. H.....October 8, 1918
CLOSNER, JOHN A., Private, Co. I.....October 8, 1918
COLE, JACK C., Private, Hq.....October 9, 1918
COOPER, EDMOND, Private, Co. A.....October 8, 1918
COOPER, LAWRENCE L., Corporal, Co. B.....October 9, 1918
COVINGTON, CLAUDE T., Private, Co. G.....October 8, 1918
COX, FOREST, Private, Co. B.....October 9, 1918
CURTIS, WILL C., Private, Co. M.....October 27, 1918
CURTIS. WILLIAM Q., Private, Co. M.....October 9, 1918
CUSHER, SIMEON, Private 1 cl., Co. E.....October 8, 1918
DEAKIN, JOHN C., Private 1 cl., Co. B.....October 9, 1918
DALE. CLEASON N., Mechanic, Co. B.....October 8, 1918
DANIEL, GEORGE M., Private, Co, G.....October 8, 1918
DUNNAWAY, MONTE E., Corporal, Co. L.....October 8, 1918
DUNN, ULIS E., Private 1 cl., Co. B.....October 9, 1918
EASTON. ROSCOE, Private 1 cl., Co. F.....October 9, 1918

EDDINGS, NOAH E., Private, Co. L.....October 8, 1918
EDWARDS. LEE R., Private, Co. G.....October 9, 1918
FINLEY, LEE S., Corporal, Co. L.....October 9, 1918
FLOYD, ANDREW M., Private, Co. G.....October 8, 1918
FOBB, EDMOND, Private 1 cl., Co. E.....October 8, 1918
FORD, GORDON F., Private, Co. I.....October 8, 1918
FOSTER, THOMAS E., Private, Co. B.....October 8, 1918
FRAZIER, GLENN, Corporal, Co. F.....October 9, 1918
FRENCH, SAMUEL T., Private, Co. I.....October 8, 1918
FRY, OSCAR L., Private, Co. K.....October 27, 1918
FULLER, BEN W., Private, Hq.....October 9, 1918
GAMMILL, ALLIE, Corporal, Co. C.....October 22, 1918
GIFFORD, CLAUDE C. Private, Co. D.....October 8, 1918
GOODBEAR, HARVEY, Private, Co. A.....October 8, 1918
GOODGER, WILLIE E., Private, Co. M.....October 9, 1918
GRAHAM, NOEL, Private, Co. L.....October 8, 1918
GRAVES, BENTON, Private, Co. L.....October 8, 1918
GRAVES, THOMAS J., Private, Co. L.....October 8, 1918
GREEN, JOHN H., Sergeant, Co. E.....October 8, 1918
HANNA, EWELL, Private, Co. M-G.....October 8, 1918
HARJO, WILLIAM S., Private, Co. M.....October 9, 1918
HANCOCK. JOHN L., Private, Co. G.....October 8, 1918
HEATH, JAMES R., Private, Co. L.....October 9, 1918
HENEISE, CHARLES W., Corporal, Co. H.....October 8, 1918
HEMMING, CHARLES G., Private 1 cl., Co. B.....October 9, 1918
HENNINGTON, JAMES M., Corporal, Co. G.....October 8, 1918
HIGNIGHT, EARL K., Sergeant, Co. E.....October 8, 1918
HILL, CHARLES P., Private, Co. F.....October 9, 1918
HILL, LON A., Corporal, Co. D.....October 8, 1918
HEDGE, ESEE, Private, Co. F.....October 8, 1918
HOLLINGSWORTH, PERCY, Private, Co. F.....October 9, 1918
HOUSTON, ROBERT A., Private, Co. C.....October 8, 1918
HOLBROOK. CLARENCE E., Private, Co. B.....October 9, 1918
HUCKABEE, LAZELLE E., Private 1 cl., Co. G.....October 8, 1918
HURST, JOHN E., Private, Co. F.....October 9, 1918
JOHNSON, JAMES O., Private, Co. B.....October 9, 1918
JONES, ESTEL L., Private, Co. G.....October 8, 1918
JONES, OKLAHOMA, Private, Co. G.....October 8, 1918
JONES, ROBERT C., Private, Co. A.....October 8, 1918
WEITH, ELMER G., Private, Co. E.....October 8, 1918
KING, ROY C., Corporal, Co. M.....October 9, 1918
LANE, JAMES W., Private, Co. F.....October 9, 1918
LANTOSCH, JOSEPH P., Private, Med. Det.....October 8, 1918
LEONARD, EARL C., Private 1 cl., Co. H.....October 8, 1918

LeROY, JOSEPH M., Private 1 cl., Co. B.....October 9, 1918
LEITZKE, JOHN F., Corporal, Co. B.....October 9, 1918
MEUNEY, ALVIN, Corporal, Co. G.....October 8, 1918
McADAMS, SAMUEL J., Private, Co. L.....October 8, 1918
McBRIDE, STEVEN A., Private 1 cl., Co. D.....October 8, 1918
McGREADY, James C., Private, Co. F.....October 8, 1918
McDANIEL, JOHN F., Sergeant, Co. G.....October 8, 1918
McFADDEN, JAMES R., Corporal, Co. L.....October 8. 1918
McGOWAN, LLOYD W., Private 1 cl., Co. G....October 8, 1918
McNITZKY, ARTHUR O., Private, Co. M.....October 9, 1918
MENDENHALL, RAY S., Private, Co. A.....October 8, 1918
MYERS, LEVI, Private, Co. L.....October 8, 1918
MINER, THOMAS L., Private, Co. K.....October 9, 1918
MIX, CHARLES, Private, Co. E.....October 9, 1918
MOORE, GILBERT, Corporal, Co. F.....October 9, 1918
MOORE, LESLIE, Private, Co. B.....October 8, 1918
MONTGOMERY, CHARLES G. P., Private 1 cl. Co. I.....October 27, 1918
MORGAN, DAVID H., Private, Co. I.....October 8, 1918
MOSS, ROBERT E., Sergeant, Co. E.....October 9, 1918
NEIL, WILLIAM J. B., Private, Co. H.....October 8, 1918
NEW, ELMER, Sergeant, Co. F.....October 9, 1918
PAGE, WILLIAM P., Private 1 cl., Co. H.....October 8, 1918
PENDLETON, JIM B., Private 1 cl., Co. H.....October 9, 1918
PERKINS, JOHN M., Private, Co. I.....October 27, 1918
PETTITT, MACK. Private, Co. H.....October 8, 1918
PIDCOCK, SAMUEL A., Private 1 cl., Co. B.....October 9, 1918
POE. ALTON C., Private 1 cl., Co. H.....October 8, 1918
POLK, ROLAND W., Corporal, Co. H.....October 8, 1918
PORTER, JONEY, Corporal, Co. L.....October 8, 1918
POWERS, ERNEST A., Corporal, Co. F.....October 8, 1918
POWERS, MARTIN L., Private, Hq.....October 8, 1918
PRICE, SAM P., Private 1 cl., Co. H.....October 8, 1918
REID, CHESTER F., Private, Co. B.....October 8, 1918
RAWIS, JESSE R., Private, Co. F.....October 9, 1918
REAGAN, FANCHER D., Sergeant, Co. M.....October 9, 1918
REEVES, BASIL O., Corporal, Co. G.....October 9, 1918
ROARK, ENIEUS I., Private, Co. A.....October 8, 1918
RODERICK, AMBERS B., Private 1 cl., Co. H.....October 8, 1918
ROGERS. PLEAS M., Private, Co. F.....October 9, 1918
ROBINSON, ALBERT E., Sergeant, Co. I.....October 27, 1918
ROPER, ROY, Corporal, Co. E.....October 8, 1918
ROSS, THOMAS F., Private, Co. H.....October 8, 1918
ROYALL. WILLIAM M., Private, Co. H.....October 8, 1918
RUSSELL, JAMES R., Private 1 cl., Co. H.....October 8, 1918
SANDERS, BEN L., Private, Co. F.....October 9, 1918

SANDERS, WILLIAM T., Corporal, Co. F.....October 9, 1918
SANDIGE, ROY N., Private, Co. O.....October 9, 1918
SCOTT, FRANK, Private, Co. E.....October 9, 1918
SCAFF, QUNTES A., Private 1 cl., Co. I.....October 9, 1918
SHIRER, ORLA E., Private, Co. L.....October 8, 1918
SIRMONS, WILLIAM L., Private, Co. A.....October 8, 1918
SMITH, EDGAR C., Private, Co. K.....October 27, 1918
SMITH, FLOYD W., Corporal, Co. L.....October 8, 1918
SMITH, THOMAS E., Private, Co. L.....October 22, 1918
SIMPSON, FLOYD E., Sergeant, Co. I.....October 9, 1918
SPIKES, JAMES A., Private, Hq.....October 9, 1918
SPIVEY, SULLIVAN R., Private, Co. G.....October 8, 1918
TEAGUE, CHARLES L., Corporal, Co. K.....October 9, 1918
THOMPSON, DELWIN A., Private, Co. B.....October 9, 1918
TIMS, EDMOND, Private, Co. D.....October 8, 1918
TUNSTALL, OLLIE B., Private, Co. G.....October 8, 1918
TURNER, FLORENCE W., Private, Co. B.....October 9, 1918
WALDROP, VERGEN X., Sergeant, Co. H.....October 8, 1918
WARREN, ROY L., Corporal, Co. H.....October 8, 1918
WATROUS, TED, Private, Co. C.....October 22, 1918
WEST, WILLIAM G., Private, Co. D.....October 9, 1918
WILLIAMS, ROBERT C., Corporal, Co. I.....October 9, 1918
VRANA, EDMOND W., Private 1 cl., Co. C.....October 9, 1918

143d Infantry

AKABAS, MAURICE W., Private 1 cl., Hq.....October 18, 1918
ANDERSON, MIKE, Private 1 cl., Co. G.....October 10, 1918
BELL, CHARLIE, Private 1 cl., Co. H.....October 9, 1918
BETHEA, CECIL G., Private 1 cl., Co. H.....October 9, 1918
BOULTINHEURSE, SCHILLIE, Private 1 cl., Co. B.....October 21, 1918
BICKLEY, JOHNNIE L., Private, Co. G.....October 10, 1918
COATES, THOMAS L., Private, Co. C.....October 14, 1918
CREPPIN, FELIX, Private, Hq.....October 8, 1918
CRIM, ROBERT L., Private 1 cl., Med. Det.....October 9, 1918
DWINELL, NORMAN E., Private 1 cl., Co. G....October 10, 1918
EHLERS, HUGE J., Private, Med. Det.....October 10, 1918
FLEMMING, BERT M., Private 1 cl., Co. C....October 14, 1918
GANTT, GEORGE E., Private, Med. Det.....October 9, 1918
GOODHUE, JAMES W., Private 1 cl., Co. L....October 9, 1918
HICK, THOMAS B., Private 1 cl., Co. G.....October 12, 1918
HINTON, ALLEN, Corporal, Co. I.....October 12, 1918
KILLEBREW, GEORGE W., Private, Co. G.....October 10, 1918
KING, WILLIAM G., Private, Co. K.....October 10, 1918
KLEMENT, CHARLES E., Private 1 cl.,.....October 10. 1918
LAKEY, GENERAL M., Sergeant, Co F.....October 27, 1918

LEWIS, SAM, Private 1 cl. Co. B.....October 21, 1918
OLLRE, JOE, Private, Co. C.....October 13, 1918
SCHROEDER, HERBERT H., Private, Co. K....October 12, 1918
SIMMONS, WILLIAM L., Private 1 cl., Med. Det.....October 9, 1918
SEWELL, CHARLIE L., Private, Med. Det.....October 9, 1918
STALLINGS, CHARLES B., Private 1 cl., Med. Det.....October 9, 1918
TARVER, ROBERT S., Corporal, Co. H.....October 9, 1918
TAYLOR, JACOB N., Private 1 cl., Co. G.....October 10, 1918
WAGNER, FELIX, Private, Co. I.....October 12. 1918

144th Infantry

ALLEN, ELIJAH F., Private, Co, A.....October 13, 1918
ALLEN, ORBA N., Private, Co. B.....October 12, 1918
AYCOCK, CLYDE A., Private, Co. D.....October 13, 1918
BASS, JAMES F., Private, Co. B.....October 10, 1918
CHRISTIAN, JOHN W., Private, Co. M.....October 13, 1918
CURRY, JOHN E., Corporal, Co. D.....October 13, 1918
DAVIS, ROBERT H., Corporal, Co. B.....October 13, 1918
ECKERT, MAX H., Private, Co. B.....October 13, 1918
EVANS, AUBREY R., Private, Co. K.....October 13, 1918
FAUST, JOHN W., Private, Co. C.....October 12, 1918
FOSTER, CLEBURN H., Private, Co. M.....October 13, 1918
GRIMES, HENRY H., Private 1 cl., Co. C.....October 13, 1918
GRIMES, JAMES S., Private 1 cl., Co. B.....October 15, 1918
HEYSER, DUNCAN B. D., Private 1 cl., Co. M.....October 13, 1918
HOLLEY, WALTER M., Private, Co. A.....October 10, 1918
JACKSON, JOHN D., Private, Co. G.....October 12, 1918
KEETER, ADEN L., Private, Co. L.....October 13, 1918
LOWERY, ANDREW J., Private, Co. M.....October 13, 1918
MANUEL, FRANK, Private, Co. M.....October 13, 1918
MILLER, GRADY M., Sergeant, Co. K.....October 13, 1918
MORGAN, LESTER, Private, Co. B.....October 13, 1918
ORCHARD, JERRE N., Private, Co. G.....October 11, 1918
PHILLIPS, IRVING B., Private, Co. B.....October 14, 1918
PRICE, GUY E., Private, Co. D.....October 13, 1918
SCHLAUDT, ALFRED J., Private 1 cl., Co. B.....October 13, 1918
SHAW, SETH S., Private, Co. M-G.....October 11, 1918
SHOCK, EVERETT G., Sergeant, Co. B.....October 13, 1918
SKAGGS, WALTER C, Private, Co. H.....October 13, 1918
SMITH, GRAHAM P., Private 1 cl., Co. D.....October 13, 1918
SPANGLER, JAMES H., Private, Co. D.....October 13, 1918
STARBUCK, GEORGE H., Corporal, Co. B.....October 14, 1918
STEELE, LINDVILLE H., Private, Co. B.....October 13, 1918
TILL, JOHN, Private, Co. B.....October 13, 1918
UNDERWOOD, LILLIARD N., Private, Co. M-G.....October 11, 1918

VANSTORY, SAM. Private, Co. L.....October 13, 1918
VEIGT, ORBIX F., Private, Co. M.....October 13, 1918
WEBB, FRANK D., Corporal, Co. B.....October 11, 1918
WILLIAMS, PAT C. Sergeant, Co. M.....October 13, 1918

133d Machine Gun Battalion

SAXDERS, MARSHALL L. Private, Co. A.....October 13, 1918

111th Field Signal Battalion

ROGERS, CHARLES J., Corporal, Co. C.....October 8, 1918

132d Machine Gun Battalion

ARANT, ALLEN B., Private 1 cl., Co. C.....October 8, 1918
ARMSTRONG. HOMER R., Private 1 cl, Co. A.....October 8, 1918
ATLAS, ALBERT, Private 1 cl., Co. A.....October 8, 1918
CARPENTER, WILLIAM H., Private 1 cl., Co. A.....October 8, 1918
COX, MARVIN F., Private 1 cl., Co. C.....October 9, 1918
EDWARDS. DEAVER W., Corporal, Co. A.....October 9, 1918
HOUSTON, LEOXARD C., Private 1 cl., Co. B.....October 8, 1918
JOHNS, GEORGE W., Sergeant, Co. C.....October 9, 1918
OWEN, TOM H., Private 1 cl., Co. C.....October 26, 1918
RISINGER, OLLIE O., Private, Co. C.....October 9, 1918
STINCHCOMB, ERNEST C., Private, Co. B.....October 8, 1918
UTTERBACK, BIRDNER E., Corporal, Co. B.....October 8, 1918
VAN OSDOL, JAMES E., Private 1 cl., Co. B.....October 8, 1918
WADE, HERBERT E., Private 1 cl., Co. C.....October 8, 1918
WALLS, EDWARD. Private, Co. A.....October 8, 1918

111th Engineers

CORNELISON, PORTER H., Private, Co. F.....November 1, 1918

Died of Wounds

111st Infantry

ALLEN, CLARENCE B., Private, Hq.....October 8, 1918
BLACKWELL, FLORENCE C., Private, Co. H.....October 9, 1918
CLAYTON, JAMES A., Private, Hq.....October 11, 1018
DEUTSCH, JOHN J., Sergeant, Co. M-G.....October 8, 1918
GAHAGAN, S. A., Private, Co. E.....October 12, 1918
GREENWOOD, C. O., Private, Co. E.....October 10, 1918
HARRIS, ALBERT L., Private, Hq.....October 11, 1918
JAYNO, W. W., Private, Co. E.....October 12, 1918

LASCH, DAVID W., Private, Co. I.....October 9, 1918
LIVESAY, JAMES R., Sergeant, Co. A.....October 17, 1918
PARKER, SAM L., Private, Co. K.....October 9, 1918
SMITH, GUSTON K., Corporal, Co. B.....October 9, 1918
WESTERMAN, WALDO A., Private, Co. M-G.....October 12, 1918

112d Infantry.

AUTRY, FITZHUGH L., 1st Sergeant, Co. F.....October 8, 1918
BOSWELL, ROY A., Private, Co. G.....October 14, 1918
COCHELL, CLELL C, Sergeant, Co. G.....October 8, 1918
DeCORDOVAN, ALLEN L., Corporal, Co. L.....October 10, 1918
DINGLER, JUDDIE V., Private 1 cl., Co. H.....October 8, 1918
DOOLEY, CLIFFORD L., Private 1 cl., Co. G.....October 8. 1918
GOOCH, GLENN, Corporal, Co. H.....October 8, 1918
GRIESON, OLIVER H., Private, Co. F.....October 9, 1918
JOHNSON, GEORGE V., Private, Hq.....November 6, 1918
NEWTON, JOHN V., Private, Hq.....October 31, 1918
PEARCE, LOUIS G., Corporal, Co. C.....October 13, 1918
RICHARDSON, BEN H, Private, Co. F.....October 8, 1918
RUSSELL, JOHN C, Private, Co. F.....October 20, 1918
SHOEMAKER, LONNE O., Corporal, Co. L.....November 11, 1918
TUNE, SAM W., Sergeant, Co. M-G.....October 9, 1918

132d Machine Gun Battalion

BUZAN, OLIVER W., Private, Co. D.....October 9, 1918
CASEY, LOUIS W., Private 1 cl., Co. D.....October 28, 1918
CLENDENNING, BENEJAH H., Private 1 cl., Co. D.....November 6, 1918
KLEIN, CHARLES, Private, Co. D.....October 28, 1918
KRAMPOTA, ANTON, Private, Co. D.....October 9, 1918
OWEN, TOM H., Private 1 cl., Co. D.....October 26, 1918
STALLINGS, RAY, Private, Co. C.....October 10, 1918
WADE, HERBERT E., Private 1 cl., Co. C.....October 8, 1918

144th Infantry

BARLOW, JOE W., Private 1 cl., Co. K.....October 15, 1918
FEAGINS, WALTER C., Corporal, Co. L.....October 21, 1918
HODEN, THOMAS, Private, Co. C.....October 12, 1918
KIRKENDALL, JOHN, Corporal, Co. M-G.....October 25, 1918
PARKS, WILLIAM, Private, Co. A.....October 26, 1918
PERTZ, MAURICIE, Private, Co. M.....October 11, 1918
REDRIQUES, JUAN M., Private, Co. B.....October 14, 1918
HINES, THOMAS, Private 1 cl., Co. M.....October 15, 1918

www.ingramcontent.com/pod-product-compliance
Lightning Source LLC
LaVergne TN
LVHW091302080426
835510LV00007B/353